PITTSBURGH REPRINT SERIES

General Editor

Dikran Y. Hadidian

2

ANSELM: FIDES QUAERENS INTELLECTUM

Anselm's Proof of the Existence of God
in the Context of his Theological Scheme

ANSELM:
FIDES QUAERENS
INTELLECTUM

*Anselm's Proof of the Existence of God
in the Context of his Theological Scheme*

KARL BARTH

SCM PRESS LTD
56 BLOOMSBURY STREET
LONDON

Respectfully dedicated to
The Venerable Faculty of Divinity of
The University of Glasgow
as a token of gratitude
for the honour of a Doctorate of Divinity
conferred on the author
18th June 1930

Translated by Ian W. Robertson
from the German *Fides Quaerens Intellectum* 2nd edition 1958,
Evangelischer Verlag A. G., Zurich, Switzerland

FIRST ENGLISH EDITION 1960
© SCM PRESS LTD 1960
PRINTED IN GREAT BRITAIN BY
THE CAMELOT PRESS LTD
LONDON AND SOUTHAMPTON

English translation © SCM Press Ltd., 1960
Reprinted by arrangement
1985, Pickwick Publications

Library of Congress Cataloging in Publication Data

Barth, Karl, 1886–1968.
  Anselm, Fides quaerens intellectum.
  (Pittsburgh reprint series ; 2)
  Reprint. Originally published: London : SCM Press, c1960.
  1. Anselm, Saint, Archbishop of Canterbury, 1033–1109. Proslogion. 2.
God—Proof, Ontological. I. Title. II. Title: Fides quaerens intellectum.
B765.A83P833   1985   212'.1   84-26578
ISBN 0-915138-75-1

Printed and Bound by Publishers Choice Book Mfg. Co.
Mars, Pennsylvania 16046

CONTENTS

ABBREVIATIONS

C.D.h.	*Cur Deus homo*
C. Gaun.	*Contra Gaunilonem* (*Responsio editoris* in Schmitt edition)
comm. op.	*Commendatio operis ad Urbanum Papam II*
De casu diab.	*De casu diaboli*
De conc. virg.	*De conceptu virginali et de originali peccato*
De concordia	*De concordia praescientiae et praedestinationis et gratiae dei cum libero arbitrio*
De lib. arb.	*De libertate arbitrii*
De nuptiis consang.	*De nuptiis consanguineorum*
De proc. Spir.	*De processione Spiritus sancti*
De verit.	*De veritate*
Ep. de incarn.	*Epistola de incarnatione verbi*
Monol.	*Monologion*
MPL	*Patrologia Latina*, ed. J.-P. Migne
Pro insip.	*Pro insipiente* (*Gaunilonis*)
Prosl.	*Proslogion*

PREFACE TO THE FIRST EDITION

THIS Preface must be devoted at least to some extent to answering the question of what I intend this book to accomplish. The question embarrasses me a little as I realize how varied have been the motives which prompted me to start and have been prompting me since I started.

First I must mention the outward cause, which in its own way was also a very inward cause, namely a seminar on Anselm's *Cur Deus homo* which I held in Bonn during the summer of 1930. The questions and objections of those who took part in this seminar and then, most important of all, a Guest Lecture by my philosopher friend Heinrich Scholz of Münster on the Proof of God's Existence in Anselm's *Proslogion*, produced within me a compelling urge to deal with Anselm quite differently from hitherto, to deal directly with the problematical Anselm, the Anselm of *Proslogion 2-4*, to establish and clarify in concrete form my own position in regard to him and to express my views on the subject to a wider circle. I may add that in this good company Heinrich Scholz decided for his part to do the same and so we are to expect from him too a study of the Anselm of *Proslogion 2-4*—doubtless a welcome counterpart to this work. It will appear in this series fairly soon.

But of course my love for Anselm goes back much further than that. In my 'Prolegomena' to the *Dogmatics* I made vigorous reference to him and as a result was promptly accused of Roman Catholicism and of Schleiermacherism.[1] The present work is not intended as a defence against that charge. However, it did seem appropriate that at some time, both for my own sake and for others, I ought to make a definite statement of some of the reasons why I find more of value and significance in this theologian than in others. I hope I may be successful in

[1] However, only because of quotations from Grabmann's book on Scholasticism, which from the theological point of view is not particularly distinguished.

7

making both sides give careful attention to him, for so far they have failed to do so. Thomas Aquinas and Kant were at one in their misunderstanding and denial of that very aspect of Anselm's theology which is to be our special concern here. One who stands on so privileged a height that this could be true of him must surely be reckoned, by Protestants and Roman Catholics alike, far more than is commonly the case, as one of those phenomena that simply must be known and respected.

Moreover, I was also interested in the mere technical aspect of the problem of interpretation which Anselm's Proof of the Existence of God had raised. About this Proof much has already been written. Its interpretation, traditional since Gaunilo and all but canonized through Thomas Aquinas and still influential even in our day,[1] always struck me as being a kind of intellectual insolence concealing or distorting everything vital. On the other hand, neither was I convinced of the value of the other interpretations that have been expounded to us in the last few decades from the widest variety of sources,[2] more subtle and more accurate as they undoubtedly are. When I looked around for the causes of my dissatisfaction the following two formal questions more or less forced themselves upon me concerning the literature to date. Is it possible to assess Anselm's Proof of the Existence of God unless it is read, understood and explained within the series of the other Anselmic Proofs, that is within the general context of his 'proving', the context of his own particular theological scheme? And is it possible to assess it without an exact exegesis of the whole passage (*Prosl. 2-4*) which is to be regarded as the main text—an exegesis that investigates every word and that also gives as full consideration as possible to Anselm's discussion with Gaunilo? I have tried to

[1] For instance, to mention only three examples—F. Chr. Baur's Account and Criticism in his *Kirchgeschichte*, Vol. 3, 1861, pp. 287f.; or Überweg-Baumgartner's *Geschichte der Philosophie*, 10th ed., 1915, vol. 2, p. 270; or J. Bainvel in vol. 1 of the *Dictionnaire de Théologie catholique*, 1923, columns 1351f.

[2] We may mention the names B. Adlhoch, R. Seeberg, K. Heim, A. Koyré, W.v.d. Steinen and of an older generation the worthy F. R. Hasse.

give effect to both these presuppositions, which up until now seem to have been left out of account as much by Anselm's critics as by his friends. Whatever position one may wish to take up with regard to the interpretation to which this path has led me, I hope that at least it will be granted that this path is in fact the right one and that even the champions of other interpretations have to start out along this same road.

From all this I cannot deny that I deem Anselm's Proof of the Existence of God in the context of his theological Scheme a model piece of good, penetrating and neat theology, which at every step I have found instructive and edifying, though I would not and could not identify myself completely with the views of its author. Moreover, I believe that it is a piece of theology that has quite a lot to say to present-day theology, both Protestant and Roman Catholic, which, quite apart from its attitude to its particular form, present-day theology ought to heed. In saying that, I may be suspected of reading this or that idea into the eleventh-century thinker, so that under the protection of his century I might advance it in the twentieth. But I have no qualms. Who can read with eyes other than his own? With that one reservation I think I am able to say that I have advanced nothing here but what I have actually read in Anselm.

As it is obvious that I have such a variety of aims in writing this book, I am entitled to hope that my reader's interest will be served, if not with all, then at least with some of them.

Bergli,
Oberrieden (Canton Zürich),
August 1931

PREFACE TO THE SECOND EDITION

IT was in the series 'Studies in the History and Doctrine of Protestantism' (Chr. Kaiser, Munich), edited by what now seems such a remarkable trio, Paul Althaus, Karl Barth and Karl Heim, that this book first appeared twenty-seven years ago. There was some very interesting criticism at the time and it seemed to me that the Roman Catholic observations were more pertinent, more reasonable and more worthy of consideration than the others. In the preface to the first edition a companion (perhaps even rival) volume to be written by my dear friend Heinrich Scholz, who died on 30th December, 1956, was promised, but unfortunately this was not to be. In such a volume he would have tackled the problem in his inimitable mathematical and logical manner and would undoubtedly have shed light both on it and also for all of us on the indefinable reality of our friendship—at the point where it was indefinable. In the meantime through pressure of other work he, like myself, had to some extent lost sight if not of Anselm's main theme, at least of the particular way in which he developed it. So far as I was concerned, after finishing this book I went straight into my *Church Dogmatics* and it has kept me occupied ever since and will continue to occupy me for the rest of my days. Only a comparatively few commentators, for example Hans Urs von Balthasar, have realized that my interest in Anselm was never a side-issue for me or—assuming I am more or less correct in my historical interpretation of St Anselm—realized how much it has influenced me or been absorbed into my own line of thinking. Most of them have completely failed to see that in this book on Anselm I am working with a vital key, if not the key, to an understanding of that whole process of thought that has impressed me more and more in my *Church Dogmatics* as the only one proper to theology. So it has come about, other circumstances probably helping as well, that to my sorrow and surprise this book, on which at the time I expended special care and devotion, has remained until now in its first edition and has long been out of print. In view of a renewed demand, particularly from the younger generation, Evangelische Verlag, Zollikon, who now handle all my pre-1938 works, decided to issue a new edition. It presents no new material. That would have meant plunging back into the texts and analysing the vociferous objections made then and since and for that I just do not have the time now. The only important change that will be found here is that the references are taken from the edition of the *Collected Works* of Anselm which has appeared in the interval (*S. Anselmi Cantuariensis Archiepiscopi Opera omnia ad fidem codicum recensuit Franciscus Salesius Schmitt, O.S.B.*, vols. I-V, 1938-1951). That is except for a few passages from less well attested writings of Anselm that are quoted here as before from Migne (*MPL*) since their reproduction is reserved pending the publication of a later volume of the new edition. The Note on Sources in the first edition is thus no longer necessary. The work involved in this revision has been carried out with skill and devotion by Mr Hinrich Stoevesandt, a divinity student, and I am grateful to him.

Basel
August, 1958

PREFACE TO THE REPRINT EDITION

KARL BARTH'S book *Anselm: Fides Quaerens Intellectum* was first published in 1931. To his sorrow and surprise, this book on which, as he said, he expended special care and devotion, remained in its first edition and was long out of print. Twenty-two years later—1958—a second German edition appeared, of which an English translation was published by the SCM Press two years later. It fared no better than the German original. Now after fifteen years, in which existentialism and the secular meaning of the Gospel seem to have run their course and ended in the dead-end street of the "death of God," and thanks to the renewed interest in theology, particularly among the younger generation, a re-print of the book that deals specifically with a *theological* proof of the *existence* of God is again available to English readers. It has been published under the auspices of the Karl Barth Society of North America by the Pickwick Publications under the editorship of Mr. Dikran Y. Hadidian, the librarian of Pittsburgh Theological Seminary.

In the *Church Dogmatics* II, 1 (1940) on the doctrine of God, Barth acknowledged that he had "learned the fundamental attitude to the problem of the knowledge and existence of God . . . at the feet of Anselm of Canterbury, and in particular from his proofs of God set out in *Proslogium* 2-4." The importance of Barth's book, however, goes far beyond providing a key to the problem of the knowledge and existence of God. In the preface to the second German edition he states that he was "working with a vital key, if not the key, to an understanding of that whole process of thought that has impressed me more and more in my *Church Dogmatics* as the only one proper to theology." That key is the epistemological principle that knowledge of God and man springs from faith in God's self-revelation in Jesus Christ and rests upon the following sequence: revelation, faith, and *then* "ut intelligam" (in order to understand)—"faith seeking understanding."

Is it not remarkable that a theologian of the 20th century, emerging from the rationalism, moralism and experientialism of the 19th century, finds that key in a theologian of the 11th century? Barth regarded his book on Anselm as the decisive turning-point in his development. It was written between the first volume of *Die Christliche Dogmatik im Entwurf* (Christian Doctrine in Outline) in 1927 and the completely revised first volume of the *Church Dogmatics* in 1932. Let us hear Barth's own description of the change he underwent during those years. It is found in an article which he wrote in 1939 at the request of the editors of *The Christian Century*, entitled, "How My Mind Has Changed In This Decade."

> In these years I have had to rid myself of the last remnants of a philosophical, i.e., anthropological (in America one says 'humanistic' or 'naturalistic') foundation and exposition of Christian doctrine. The real document of this farewell is, in truth, not the much-read brochure *Nein!* directed against Brunner in 1934, but rather the book about the evidence for God of Anselm of Canterbury which appeared in 1931. Among all my books I regard this as the one written with the greatest satisfaction. . . . The positive factor in the new development was this: in these years I had to learn that Christian doctrine, if it is to merit its name and if it is to build up the Christian Church in the world as she must needs be built up, has to be exclusively and conclusively the doctrine of Jesus Christ—of Jesus Christ as the living Word of God spoken to us men. If I look back from this point on my earlier studies, I may well ask myself how it ever came about that I did not learn this much sooner and accordingly speak it out. How slow is man, above all when the most important things are at stake! . . . My new task was to take all that has been said before and to think it through once more and freshly and to articulate it anew as a theology of the grace of God in Jesus Christ.

In addition to the importance of the key Barth discovered in Anselm for theological methodology, the concluding paragraph of his book should continue to whet the interest of theologians and philosophers alike.

That Anselm's proof of the existence of God has repeatedly been called the 'ontological' proof of God, that commentators have refused to see that it is in a different book altogether from the well-known teaching of Descartes and Leibniz, that anyone could seriously think that it is even remotely affected by what Kant put forward against these doctrines—all that is so much nonsense on which no more words ought to be wasted.

The Karl Barth Society of North America   is proud to present Barth's *Lieblingsbuch* as hopefully the first in a series of re-prints of his works by Pickwick Publications.

Arthur C. Cochrane
President

April, 1975

INTRODUCTION

THE PROOF of the Existence of God comprises the first and dis-
proportionately shorter of the two parts (*cap. 2-4* and *5-26*) of
Anselm's *Proslogion*. The second and longer part goes on to deal
with the Nature of God. The purpose behind this arrangement
of the book is quite obvious: *Da mihi ut, quantum scis expedire,
intelligam quia es, sicut credimus et hoc es quod credimus*[1]—thus
begins the exposition proper after the great introductory
invocation of *Prosl. 1*. Before this the Prologue of the book had
described how the author had long sought and, after many a
digression, eventually found *unum argumentum . . . ad astruendum,
quia Deus vere est et quia est summum bonum*.[2] Now this *argumentum*
must not be identified with the proof which is worked out in
Prosl. 2-4 but rather it is one technical element which Anselm
has made use of in both parts of the book. Therefore, all that
he can have meant by it is the formula for describing God, by
means of which he has in fact proved the Existence of God in the
first part and the Nature of God in the second part: *Id quo maius
cogitari non potest*.[3] The sub-title *De Existentia Dei* which appears
in some manuscripts, is due to a mistaken identity, caused, as
Gaunilo's reply shows, by the tremendous impression that the
short first part made on the very earliest readers. Anselm never
meant that the part should thus be taken for the whole. The
joy he speaks of in the Prologue sprang from the discovery of
the formula by which he considered himself to be in a position
to prove, on the one hand: *quia es, sicut credimus* (with the result:
vere es); and on the other hand: *quia hoc es, quod credimus* (with
the result: *summum bonum es*). So far as he is concerned *Prosl,
5-26* is in actual fact no less important than *Prosl. 2-4*. However.

[1] *Prosl. 2*: I 101, 3f.   [2] I 93, 6ff.
[3] In Classical and Mediaeval Latin *argumentum* can mean either *terminus medius*
(middle term), *lumen quo manifestantur principia* (means of proof) or *argumentatio*
(proof set forth).

13

the aim of our inquiry should be confined to these three first chapters—the celebrated Proof of the Existence of God.

What has to be said in explanation of the Proof will only make sense if we may assume a firm grasp of what 'to prove' means in Anselm generally. Too much has been said about this proof, for it and against it, without there being any real appreciation of what Anselm was trying to do, and in fact doing, when he explained 'was proving' and when he justified this particular proof. What is set out in *Prosl.* *2-4* is first described as a 'proof' (*probare, probatio*) by Anselm's opponent Gaunilo,[1] but this designation is adopted by Anselm himself.[2] This concept can be found elsewhere in Anselm but always in passages where he is speaking of a definite result that his work has actually produced or is expected to produce. Anselm is bent on this result and strives to achieve it. But in point of fact his own particular description of what he is doing is not *probare* at all but *intelligere*. As *intelligere* is achieved it issues in *probare*. Here we can give a general definition: what to prove means is that the validity of certain propositions advocated by Anselm is established over against those who doubt or deny them; that is to say, it means the polemical-apologetic result of *intelligere*. How exactly he conceived this result and what he did and did not anticipate from it, can be ascertained only after detailed analysis of his thoughts on *intelligere*, that is to say, of his theological scheme. Therefore it is to these that we must first of all turn.

[1] *Pro insip. 1:* I 125, 4 and 7.
[2] *C. Gaun. 10:* I 138, 29; 139, 2. Anselm's 'work' *Contra Gaunilonem* ought sometime to be specially studied from the standpoint of its literary character. I regard it as probably being a collection of notes written down in two sections: 1-4, 5-10.

I

THE THEOLOGICAL SCHEME

1. THE NECESSITY FOR THEOLOGY

OUR first inquiry is into the 'necessity' by which *intelligere* becomes a problem for Anselm. It would not be wrong to make the obvious reference to the purpose of the polemical-apologetic Proof but it would merely be scratching the surface.

It ought to be noticed first of all that this is not the only result of *intelligere* that all the way through Anselm recognizes and has before him. As *intelligere* is achieved, it issues—in joy.[1] The dominating factor in Anselm's mind is that even the Church Fathers wrote about it in order to give the faithful joy in believing by a demonstration of the *ratio* of their faith.[2] This reason, which the *intelligere* seeks and finds, possesses in itself not only *utilitas* (by which Anselm may have been thinking of a polemical proof) but also *pulchritudo*. It is *speciosa super intellectus hominum*.[3] Is it mere coincidence that in a work like *Cur Deus homo*, which on its own admission is so set on proving, its chief end should be given as, first, this *delectari* and, secondly, the polemical obligation of I Peter 3.15?[4] It is evident here that a strong foundation is combined with a genial inclination to please, and this fact may well remind us that early Scholasticism

---

[1] *Ad magnum et delectabile quiddam me subito perduxit haec mea meditatio* (*Monol. 6:* I 19, 15). *Cum ad intellectum valet pertingere, delectatur* (*Ep. 136:* III 281, 40).

[2] *Ad pascendum eos, qui iam corde fide mundato fidei ratione . . . delectantur* (*C.D.h. comm. op.:* II 39, 4ff).

[3] *C.D.h. I 1:* II 48, 8f.; 49, 19. Incidentally, we learn here that Anselm was always capable of righteous indignation—over bad pictures of Christ. It may also be noted here that it is in *Prosl. 2* of all places that a *pictor* comes forward as chief witness for the relationship between the *esse rei in intellectu* and the *intelligere rem esse*.

[4] *C.D.h. I 1:* II 47, 9; cf. also *II 15:* II 116, 12: *ut me . . . intellectu laetifices.*

was contemporary with the heyday of the Romanesque style of cathedral art. And it might well be a first test of our understanding of Anselm to ask ourselves whether we are capable of appreciating that the despair with which, as he says[1] in the prologue of the *Proslogion*, he sought that *unum argumentum*, could not be taken less seriously, because in addition to the fighting spirit obviously indispensable to one engaged on theological work, he still had some freedom left to admit other spirits, one of them clearly being the aesthetics of theological knowledge. And indeed why not? Why not just that? At least we have to take this second aim of Anselm's *intelligere* very seriously and we cannot evade the prior question—what exactly does 'to prove' mean, if it is the result of the same action which may also lead straight to *delectatio*?

However, the necessity of Anselm's *intelligere* does not lie in the desirability of these, its two results. And it is only by virtue of its necessity on a higher level that these, its results, are possible and desirable. Anselm's concern in all his writings (with one exception)[2] is theology, the *intellectus fidei*. *Fides quaerens intellectum*—that was the original title of the *Proslogion*, as is made clear by the Prologue. Thus the only *intelligere* that concerns Anselm is that 'desired' by faith. And the necessity that leads us to the *intelligere* to which he is referring, and also to its results—*probare* and *laetificare*—is precisely this 'desire' of faith.

The first thing to be emphasized is the negation that this involves. What we are speaking of is a spontaneous desire of faith. Fundamentally, the *quaerere intellectum* is really immanent in *fides*. Therefore it is not a question of faith 'requiring' the 'proof' or the 'joy'. There is absolutely no question at all of a requirement of faith. Anselm wants 'proof' and 'joy' because he wants

---

[1] Cf. also *C.D.h. Preface*: II 42, 6: *in magna . . . cordis tribulatione*.

[2] Anselm himself explicitly characterized the work *De grammatico* as non-theological (*De verit. Prologue*: I 173, 5ff). Note that in the same place he represents *De veritate* as a theological work, although to us it is purely logical or metaphysical.

intelligere and he wants *intelligere* because he believes.[1] Any reversal of this order of compulsion is excluded by Anselm's conception of faith. That is to say, for Anselm, 'to believe' does not mean simply a striving of the human will towards God but a striving of the human will into God and so a participation (albeit in a manner limited by creatureliness) in God's mode of Being[2] and so a similar participation in God's aseity, in the matchless glory of his very Self, and therefore also in God's utter absence of necessity.[3] Thus on no account can the given-ness or non-given-ness of the results of *intelligere* involve for faith the question of its existence. Therefore, the aim of theology cannot be to lead men to faith,[4] nor to confirm them in the faith,[5] nor even to deliver their faith from doubt.[6] Neither does the man who asks theological questions ask them for the sake of the existence of his faith; his theological answers, however complete they may be, can have no bearing on the existence of his faith. *Gratia Dei praeveniente*, he is so sure of his faith that, so far as he is aware, *nihil tamen sit quod ab eius firmitate evellere valeat*, even although what he believes he could conceive *nulla ratione*.

[1] *Nos vero, quia credimus (rationem quaerimus) (C.D.h. I 3:* II 50, 19).

[2] *Quisquis tendendo ad illam (sc. summam essentiam) pervenerit, non extra illam remanebit, sed intra illam permanebit; quod expressius et familiarius significatur, si dicitur tendendum esse in illam, quam si dicitur ad illam. Hac itaque ratione puto congruentius posse dici credendum esse in illam quam ad illam (Monol. 76:* I 83, 27–84, 2).

[3] *Deus nihil facit necessitate, quia nullo modo cogitur aut prohibetur facere aliquid (C.D.h. II 5:* II 100, 20f). *Deus nulli quicquam debet, sed omnis creatura illi debet; et ideo non expedit homini, ut agat cum Deo, quemadmodum par cum pari (ibid. I 19:* II 86, 7ff). *Summas veritas . . . nulli quicquam debet; nec ulla ratione est quod est, nisi quia est (De verit. 10:*. I 190, 4).

[4] *Neque enim quaero intelligere, ut credam . . . (Prosl. 1:* I 100, 18). *Non ut per rationem ad fidem accedant (C.D.h. I 1:* II 47, 8; cf. *Ep. 136:* III 281, 38f).

[5] *Non ut me in fide confirmes (C.D.h. II 15:* II 116, 11). Anselm makes an urgent plea that we should not ascribe to him the dreadful *praesumptio* that he is speaking *ad confirmandum fidei Christianae firmamentum, quasi mea indigeat defensione.* That would be like trying to support Mount Olympus with pegs and ropes. Quite absurd. And here the reference is to the rock in Nebuchadnezzar's vision which tore itself away from the mountain and ended by filling the whole world. All *sancti et sapientes, qui super eius aeternam firmitatem se stabilitos esse gaudent*, would most certainly condemn me, *si eum meis rationibus fulcire et quasi nutantem stabilire nitar (Ep. de incarn. 1:* II 5, 7ff).

[6] *Non ad hoc veni, ut auferas mihi fidei dubitationem (C.D.h. I 25:* II 96, 6). He decides to come to the aid of those labouring under certain dogmatic difficulties *etiam si fides in illis superet rationem quae illis fidei videtur repugnare (Ep. de incarn. 1:* II 6, 2f).

The *rei veritas* remains fixed whatever its relation to the *intellectus ad eam capiendam*.[1] It is the presupposition of all theological inquiry that faith as such remains undisturbed by the vagaries of the theological 'yes' and 'no'.[2] If *intelligere* does not reach its goal (and it is certainly a long way from doing so), then in place of the joy of knowing there remains reverence before Truth itself, which is no less Truth because this is so.[3] For as truth, that is the validity of the propositions of human knowledge, is entirely determined by the thing believed, so is this thing (meaning faith in this thing) utterly and completely independent of the validity of these human propositions.[4]

It is not the existence of faith, but rather—and here we approach Anselm's position—the nature of faith, that desires knowledge. *Credo ut intelligam*[5] means: It is my very faith itself that summons me to knowledge. There are four separate but converging lines in Anselm's thought along which this inner compulsion becomes clear.

1. There is a neat statement of Anselm's doctrine of God that must be mentioned. It reads: *Deum veritatem esse credimus*.[6] Truth generally means: *Rectitudo mente sola perceptibilis*.[7] But God is related to all that is called Truth apart from him, not only as *summa veritas* but, because he is the Creator, also as *causa veritatis*. Thus God is at least also *causa veritatis, quae cogitationis est*.[8] He is the God in whom *intelligentia* and *veritas* are identical, the God[9] whose Word to us is nothing other than the

---

[1] *C.D.h. I 1:* II 48, 16-49, 2. *Saepe namque aliquid esse certi sumus et tamen hoc ratione probare nescimus (ibid. II 13:* II 113, 17f). *Cuncta, quae ipse (sc. Deus) dicit, certa esse . . . dubitandum non est, quamvis non eorum ratio intelligatur a nobis (ibid. II 15:* II 116, 5f). *Credentem me fecisti scire, quod nesciens credebam (De casu diab. 16:* I 261, 25).

[2] *Nulla difficultas aut impossibilitas intelligendi valeat illum a veritate, cui per fidem adhaesit, excutere (Ep. de incarn. 1:* II 10, 15f).

[3] *Cum ad intellectum valet pertingere, delectatur; cum vero nequit, quod capere non potest, veneratur (Ep. 136:* III 281, 40f). Anselm explicitly says that one of his purposes in writing the *Monologion* and the *Proslogion* was *ad adiuvandum religiosum studium eorum, qui humiliter quaerunt intelligere, quod firmissime credunt (Ep. de incarn. 6:* II 21, 2f).

[4] *Rectitudo . . . qua significatio recta dicitur, non habet esse aut aliquem motum per significationem, quomodocumque ipsa moveatur significatio. (De verit. 13:* I 198, 18ff).

[5] *Prosl. 1:* I 100, 18.   [6] *De verit. 1:* I 176, 4.   [7] *Ibid., 11:* I 191, 19f.
[8] *Ibid., 10:* I 190. 10f.   [9] *Monol. 46:* I 62, 20ff.

integra veritas paternae substantiae.[1] He is *sensibilis*, that is, *cognoscibilis*.[2] Obviously we cannot believe in this God without his becoming the author of a *vera cogitatio*—that is, faith in him also demands knowledge of him.

2. According to Anselm's psychology, faith is in effect primarily a movement of the will. We heard earlier of the paraphrase: *tendere in Deum*.[3] This *tendere*, however, is nothing but the voluntary decision of obedience owed to God—love for God.[4] But to this effective primacy of the will there corresponds the original primacy of knowledge.[5] Faith means the free exercise of will, but an exercise of will by a rational creature means choosing and depends on the distinction between *iustum et iniustum, verum et non verum, bonum et malum*.[6] This distinguishing is clearly the basic act of what we call knowing.

3. The relation with which we are at present dealing can also be understood from the side of Anselm's anthropology. Faith, according to Anselm, does not come about without something new encountering us and happening to us from outside, *nequaquam sine sui generis semine et laboriosa cultura. Fides esse nequit sine conceptione.* The seed to be received is the 'Word of God' that is preached and heard; and that it comes to us and that we have the *rectitudo volendi* to receive it, is grace.[7] But the Word encounters in us a *potestas*—Anselm describes it as the *imago summae essentiae* (of the holy Three-in-One-ness of God) *per*

---

[1] *Ibid., 46:* I 62, 25f.   [2] *Prosl. 6:* I 104f.   [3] *Monol. 76f:* I 83f.

[4] *Sicut Deus volunte bonus est, sic homo, ad eius similitudinem factus, volunte bonus . . . quia imitatur eum qui aeternaliter et essentialiter a se ipso est bonus (Medit. 19:* 5, MPL 158, 806f). *Nihil igitur apertius quam rationalem creaturam ad hoc esse factam, ut summam essentiam amet super omnia bona (Monol. 68:* I 79, 1ff). So too, the concept *veritas* receives its ultimate and crucial interpretation by the concept *justitia,* that is: *rectitudo voluntatis propter se servata (De verit. 12:* I 194, 26).

[5] *Amare autem eam nequit, nisi eius reminisci et eam studuerit intelligere (Monol. 68:* I 79, 5f). *Iustitia cui laus debetur* (as. distinct from the righteousness of irrational creatures) *. . . non est in ulla natura, quae rectitudinem non agnoscit . . . Velle autem illam non valet, qui nescit eam (De verit. 12:* I 192, 27-33). And right on to eternal blessedness it holds true that: *Utique tantum gaudebunt, quantum amabunt; tantum amabunt, quantum cognoscent (Prosl. 26:* I 121, 9f).

[6] *Monol. 68:* I 78, 22; *C.D.h. II 1:* II 97, 6.

[7] *De concordia Qu. III 6:* II 270, 20f; 271, 7ff.

naturalem potentiam impressa—by which, without participation in them, we are yet capable of (a) recollection of, (b) knowledge of and (c) love for an *optimum et maximum omnium*. It is this *potestas*, this *vestigium trinitatis*, that distinguishes us from animals and makes us men.[1] In faith this potentiality is actualized.[2] Although man does not believe apart from the Word that comes to him and apart from prevenient grace—the *imago Dei* instead of being *naturaliter impressa* is now *per voluntarium effectum expressa*[3]—nevertheless, (a) he 'remembers'[4] God, (b) he recognizes God and (c) he loves God. Knowledge of God must then come about, like love to God, on the occurrence of faith, because the completeness of man's likeness to God, as restored in the Christian, so requires it.

4. The fourth line in Anselm along which *intelligere* necessarily follows from faith is the line of eschatology. On one occasion he called the *intellectus, quem in hac vita capimus* the *medium inter fidem et speciem*.[5] We ought not to press his reasoning here too far for it is obviously a little vague. For him knowledge, as opposed to vision, ranks higher than faith only in a very relative sense.[6] There can be absolutely no question at all of *intelligere* breaking through the barrier between the *regnum gratiae* and the *regnum gloriae*. On the contrary, it is in its very *quaerere* and *invenire* that *intellectus* comes up against the inexorable limitations of humanity in a way that faith, as such, does not. Just because he is *intelligens* the Christian, of all men, has to learn to discern with agonizing clarity what is conceivable by him about

---

[1] *Monol. 32:* I 51, 9ff; *67:* I 78, 7ff; *68:* I 79, Iff.

[2] *Creasti in me hanc imaginem tuam, ut tui memor te cogitem, te amem. Sed sic est abolita attritione vitiorum, sic est offuscata fumo peccatorum, ut non possit facere ad quod facta est, nisi tu renoves et reformes eam (Prosl. I:* I 100, 12ff).

[3] *Monol. 68:* I 78, 15f.

[4] As far as I am aware Anselm made no further use of the doctrine of the *memoria*, which was undoubtedly taken over from Augustine (*Confessions* x 17 to 24). At any rate, in contrast to Augustine, he did not develop the idea in a Platonic or Neo-Platonic way.

[5] *C.D.h. comm. op.:* II 40, 10f.

[6] It is better to avoid this kind of distinction of value in Anselm.

God himself.[1] So we shall have to interpret the medial character of knowledge in Anselm's sense by saying that knowledge stands between faith and vision in the same way as we might say that a mountain stands between a man looking at it from the valley and the sun. *Intelligere* is a potentiality for advancing in the direction of heavenly vision to a point that can be reached and that is worth trying to reach. It has within itself something of the nature of vision and it is worth striving for as *similitudo* of vision, just because it leads men, not beyond, but right up to the limits of faith.[2]

This is the *ratio* of *credo ut intelligam*—independent of all objectives and so of all attempts at proving or at finding joy: the God in whom we believe is *causa veritatis in cogitatione*. Knowledge at once combines with that love of God on which faith is set. *Intellectus* is also involved in actualizing the *imago Dei* as this occurs in faith. *Intellectus* is the limited, but fully attainable, first step towards that vision which is the eschatological counterpart of faith. Therefore *fides* is essentially—*quaerens intellectum*. Therefore Anselm regards it as *negligentia, si postquam confirmati sumus in fide, non studemus, quod credimus, intelligere*.[3] Therefore just because we possess the certainty of faith, we must hunger after the *fidei ratio*.[4]

[1] *Adhuc lates, Domine, animam meam in luce et beatitudine tua, et idcirco versatur illa adhuc in tenebris et miseria sua (Prosl. 17: I 113, 7f). Ergo, Domine, non solum es quo maius cogitari nequit, sed es quiddam maius quam cogitari possit (Prosl. 15: I 112, 13f). Cur non te sentit, Domine Deus, anima mea, si invenit te? An non invenit, quem invenit esse lucem et veritatem? Quomodo namque intellexit hoc, nisi videndo lucem et veritatem? Aut potuit omnino aliquid intelligere de te nisi per lucem tuam et veritatem tuam? . . . An et veritas et lux est quod vidit, et tamen nondum te vidit, quia vidit te aliquatenus, sed non vidit te sicuti es? Domine Deus meus, formator et reformator meus, dic desideranti animae meae, quid aliud es quam quod vidit, ut pure videat quod desiderat (Prosl. 14: I 111, 14-24).*

[2] *Plus enim persuadebis altiores in hac re rationes latere, si aliquam te videre monstraveris, quam si te nullam in ea rationem intelligere nihil dicendo probaveris (C.D.h. II 16: II 117, 20ff).*

[3] *C.D.h. I 1:* II 48, 17f.

[4] *Fidei rationem post eius (sc. fidei) certudinem debemus esurire (C.D.h. comm. op.:* II 39, 5)—an injunction (*intentionem ad intellectum extendere*), which Anselm along with Augustine found explicitly stated in the *nisi credideritis non intelligetis*, the famous misunderstanding of Isa. 7.9.

2. THE POSSIBILITY OF THEOLOGY

When we ask ourselves how an *intellectus fidei* is possible at all and how the formula *credo ut intelligam* is feasible, there is one overriding consideration to be kept in mind. For Anselm, as well as for the whole of the Early Church (including the Reformation and Protestant orthodoxy), the actual *credere* itself was never an illogical, irrational and, in respect of knowledge, wholly deficient *tendere in Deum*, in spite of the continual emphasis on its distinctive character as obedience and experience. Inasmuch as faith is faith in God,[1] and therefore really faith in what is right, it is the proper action of the will— due to God, enjoined by God and bound up with saving 'experience'. Faith comes by hearing and hearing comes by preaching.[2] Faith is related to the 'Word of Christ' and is not faith if it is not conceived, that is acknowledged and affirmed by the Word of Christ. And the Word of Christ is identical with the 'Word of those who preach Christ';[3] that means it is legitimately represented by particular human words.[4] Anselm's view as to the precise extent of this human word, the authentic representative of the Word, is not very clear. But it is certain that it would include the Bible in a very special way.[5] But the

---

[1] *Amare autem aut sperare non potest, quod non credit. Expedit itaque eidem humanae animae summam essentiam et ea, sine quibus illa amari non potest, credere, ut illa credendo tendat in illam (Monol. 76:* 1 83, 16ff). *In illam tendere nisi credat illam, nullus potest (ibid. 77:* 1 84, 11f).

[2] *Didici in schola Christiana quod teneo, tenendo assero, asserendo amo (Ep. 49:* III 162, 22f).

[3] *Nullus namque velle potest, quod prius corde non concipit. Velle autem credere, quod est credendum, est recte velle. Nemo ergo potest hoc velle, si nescit, quod credendum est.* Think of Rom. 10.13-14, 17. *Quod autem (sc. Paulus) dicit fidem esse ex auditu, intelligendum est quia fides est ex hoc, quod concipit mens per auditum; neque ita, ut sola conceptio mentis faciat fidem in homine, sed quia fides esse nequit sine conceptione . . . 'Auditus autem est per verbum Christi', hoc est per verbum praedicantium Christum (De concordia Qu. III 6:* II 270, 28-271, 10).

[4] *Eorum auctoritas quibus dictum est: Non enim vos estis, qui loquimini, sed spiritus patris vestri loquitur in vobis* Matt. 10.20 (*De nuptiis consang. 1: MPL* 158, 557).

[5] He described his writings (in a paraphrase of our word 'theological') as

concept 'Holy Scripture' is itself, according to Anselm, to be understood in a fundamentally broad sense: at all events those inferences that are consistent with its text join the text with equal weight and authority.[1] And the kind of inference he was thinking of is at least partly clear. Anselm has more than once very solemnly affirmed his 'faith' in the *Symbolum Romanum*, in the *Symbolum Nicaeno-Constantinopolitanum* and in the *Symbolum Quicumque*,[2] and at the same time given great latitude for the adoption of further necessary elements of faith that are still outside formulated dogma.[3] He also made explicit and emphatic mention of the *scripta catholicorum patrum et maxime beati Augustini*, as the norm, if not the source, of his thinking.[4] And he declared that in the end the 'surest' way to refute an error theologically within the Church is to refer it (*ostendere*) to the Pope at Rome, *ut eius prudentia examinetur*.[5] In short, there now emerges the

---

tractatus pertinentes ad studium sacrae scripturae (*De verit.* Preface: I 173, 2). In passages mentioned later, in which he comes to speak of the final criterion by which he regulated all his work, in so far as he ever gave it a name, he called it Holy Scripture. In an epistolary instruction on 'The Holy Life' he urged upon the questioner the *cura studendi in sacra scriptura* as primary and fundamental (*Ep. 2:* III 99, 28). The essence of his view on the importance of Holy Scripture as the source of the Church's proclamation, he gave as follows: *Sicut ergo Deus in principio per miraculum fecit frumentum et alia de terra nascentia ad alimentum hominum sine cultore et seminibus: ita sine humana doctrina mirabiliter fecit corda prophetarum et apostolorum necnon et evangelia foecunda salutaribus seminibus: unde accipimus quidquid salubriter in agricultura Dei ad alimentum animarum seminamus, sicut non nisi de primis terrae seminibus habemus, quod ad nutrimentum corporum propagamus. Siquidem nihil utiliter ad salutem spiritualem praedicamus, quod sacra scriptura Spiritus sancti miraculo foecundata non protulerit* (*De concordia Qu. III 6:* II 271, 20ff).

1 *Quare non tantum suscipere cum certitudine debemus, quae in sacra Scriptura leguntur, sed etiam ea, quae ex his, nulla alia contradicente ratione rationabili necessitate sequuntur* (*De proc. Spir. 11:* II 209, 14ff).

2 *Ep. 136:* III 280, 17ff and *Ep. de incarn. 4* (in the *Prior Recensio*, discovered and first printed by Father Schmitt). In this second passage Anselm adds: *Haec est petra, super quam aedificavit Christus ecclesiam suam, adversus quam portae inferi non praevalebunt. Haec est illa firma petra, super quam sapiens aedificavit domum suam; quae nec impulsu fluminum nec flatu ventorum est mota. Super hanc nitar aedificare domum meam. Qui aedificat super firmitatem huius fidei, aedificat super Christum; et qui non aedificat super hanc fidem, non aedificat super Christum, praeter quem fundamentum aliud poni non potest* (I 283, 15ff).

3 *Scimus enim quod non omnia, quae credere et confiteri debemus, ibi dicta sunt; nec illi, qui symbolum illud dictaverunt, voluerunt fidem Christianam esse contentam ea tantummodo credere et confiteri, quae ibi posuerunt* (*De proc. Spir. 13:* II 211, 18ff).

4 *Ep. 77:* III 199, 17ff; *Monol. Prologue:* I 8, 8ff.   5 *Ep. de incarn. 1:* II 3, 7ff.

Church[1] either as a virtual second source alongside Holy Scripture or simply as a norm for the interpretation of Scripture. If the latter, with what degree of authority? And what is the order of precedence of the various elements—Dogma, Tradition, Fathers, Pope? These questions cannot be answered from the texts of Anselm—it must be remembered that we are in the eleventh century and not the sixteenth or the twentieth and we must not expect to find either the present-day Roman Catholic thesis or our own Protestant anti-thesis. To that extent it is not possible to give concrete definition to what Anselm understood by the *verbum praedicantium Christum*. But whatever it may be, Anselm's subjective *credo* has an objective *Credo* of the Church as its unimpeachable point of reference—that is, a number of propositions formulated in human words (including, of course, the Bible and the Symbols of the Early Church as basic documents of the Catholic Church's faith). The 'Word of Christ' is the truth that faith believes it to be, in that it is identical with the 'Word of those who preach Christ.' In relation to this human word of Christian proclamation, *credere* is the presupposition of *intelligere*.

It is just this relationship between *credo* and *Credo* that determines how far a Christian can advance from *credere* to *intelligere*, how far therefore theology is possible: As *credere* of the *Credo*, faith is itself, so to speak, an *intelligere*, distinguished from the *intelligere* which it 'desires' only in degree and not in kind.[2] In its grasp of the Christian message faith is assuredly nothing less than the awareness of a *vox significans rem*, of a coherent continuity that is expressed logically and grammatically, which, having been heard, is understood and now exists *in intellectu*. Faith of course possesses this awareness in common with unbelief. And unbelief means simply that nothing but this

---

[1] *Hic enim me querat qui quaerere vult* (*Hom. 7: MPL* 158, 629). Alongside the advice to obey (*obedire*) this first authority (Scripture), other advice is also given: *Ecclesiae sequi consuetudinem, cuius consuetudines velle convellere, genus est haeresis* (*De nuptiis consang.: MPL* 158, 557). *Quod catholica ecclesia corde credit et ore confitetur*—cannot in any circumstances be denied (*Ep. de incarn. 1:* II 6, 10f).

[2] *Adiuva me, ut intelligam, quod dico* (*Prosl. 9:* I 108, 8f).

awareness, this *esse in intellectu*, results from hearing the Christian proclamation and that the *vox significans rem* does its work in vain because the man is not aware of the *res* that it signifies.[1] Faith is also this awareness. Its affinity to *intelligere* is, however, not just this primitive and ambiguous affinity. Far above and beyond this awareness—to the *esse in intellectu* is added the *intelligere esse in re*—faith is assent to what is preached as the Truth, assent for the sake of Christ who is its real and ultimate Author and who, himself the Truth, can proclaim only the Truth.[2] If that is where it begins, this is where it ends—the ultimate in knowledge, already anticipated in faith, the final word of knowledge which (with the first word) faith has already heard—*voluntas Dei numquam est irrationabilis*.[3] If *fides quaerit intellectum*,[4] then all that remains to be considered is the gap separating this awareness that has come about and the assent which has been given. And just because the beginning and the end are already given in faith, and because all that has to be settled regarding the *intelligere* that we are seeking is the gap between these two extremes, this *intelligere* is a soluble problem and theology a feasible task. Because of this twofold affinity between *credere* and *intelligere*, Anselm is perfectly able, as opportunity affords, to describe the *obedire auctoritati* and the *sequi ecclesiae consuetudinem* in and by itself as the *simplex et pura ratio*, not merely as *auctoritas solo imperio cognoscens*, but as *ratio rationabiliter docens* of a particular proposition whose meaning is in question.[5] Anselm always has the solution of his problems

---

[1] Cf. *Prosl. 2:* I 101, 7ff and especially *4:* I 103, 18ff.

[2] *Ipse idem Deus-homo novum condat testamentum et vetus approbet: sicut ipsum veracem esse necesse est confiteri, ita nihil, quod in illis continetur, verum esse potest aliquis diffiteri* (*C.D.h. II 22:* II 133, 8ff).

[3] *C.D.h. I 8:* II 59, 11. *Nec aliquatenus quod dixit esse verum aut quod fecit, rationabiliter esse factum dubito* (*ibid. II 15:* II 116, 8f).

[4] In this connection note the final sentence of the Proof, *Prosl. 2-4: Qui ergo intelligit sic esse Deum, nequit eum non esse cogitare* (*Prosl. 4:* I 104, 4).

[5] *De nuptiis consang. 1: MPL* 158, 557. Cf. also the passage *De casu diab. 21* (I 267, 17f): *Fateor enim nondum alicubi, excepta divina auctoritate, cui indubitanter credo, me legisse rationem, quae mihi sufficeret.* Moreover, even in the *auctoritas* he found a *ratio* and no doubt a satisfying one.

25

already behind him (through faith in the impartial good sense of the decisions of ecclesiastical authority), while, as it were, they are still ahead. Therefore, his *credo ut intelligam* can as little imply an intellectual storming of the gates of heaven as it can a *sacrificium intellectus*. It is just this same objective *Credo* which compels Christian humility before the *ratio veritatis* that is the presupposition of all human knowledge of heavenly things and that belongs to the actual revelation of God. And this *Credo* makes the science of theology possible and gives it a basis. It is thus and only thus that the characteristic absence of crisis in Anselm's theologizing can be understood.[1]

3. THE CONDITIONS OF THEOLOGY

This demand on *intelligere* that we have been discussing, which *fides* both makes and meets, gives rise to a series of conditions to which theological work is subject and of which we must now speak before taking up the question of the content of theology's distinctive task.

1. In its relation to the *Credo*, theological science, as science of the *Credo*, can have only a positive character.[2] *Nam et hoc credo, quia nisi credidero, non intelligam.*[3] That is to say: While I believe, I also believe that the knowledge for which I seek, as it is demanded and rendered possible by faith, has faith as its presupposition, and that in itself it would immediately become impossible were it not the knowledge of faith.[4] Faith, however, is related to the *Credo* of the Church into which we are baptized. Thus the knowledge that is sought cannot be anything but an extension and explication of that acceptance of the *Credo* of

---

[1] It goes without saying that Anselm's *credo ut intelligam* is completely out of place on the title-page of Schleiermacher's *Glaubenslehre*.

[2] *Dedisti semper humilem scientiam, quae aedificet* (*Medit. 18: MPL* 158, 799). Theology is a *humilis sapientia* in contrast to an *insipiens superbia* (*Ep. de incarn. 1:* II 6, 8f).

[3] *Prosl. 1* (I 100, 19).

[4] *Rectus ordo exigit, ut profunda Christianae fidei prius credamus, quam ea praesumamus ratione discutere* (*C.D.h. I 1:* II 48, 16f).

the Church, which faith itself already implied. The man who asks for Christian knowledge asks, 'to what extent is it thus?', on the basis of a presupposition that is never for a moment questioned, namely, that it is as he, a Christian, believes. That and that alone. A science of faith, which denied or even questioned the Faith (the *Credo* of the Church), would *ipso facto* cease to be either 'faithful' or 'scientific'. Its denials would *a priori* be no better than bats and owls squabbling with eagles about the reality of the beams of the midday sun. *Intelligere*, the *intelligere* for which faith seeks, is compatible with a reverent 'I do not yet know' or with an ultimate ignorance concerning the extent of the truth accepted in faith. But it is not compatible with an insolent 'I know better' in face of the 'that . . .' of this truth.[1] *Intelligere* comes about by reflection on the *Credo* that has already been spoken and affirmed.[2]

2. The theologian asks—'to what extent is reality as the Christian believes it to be?' Anselm did not deny that this question of degree, if pushed beyond a certain limit, would be turned into a question of fact and so theology would be turned into 'a-theology'. For that reason the question may not be pushed beyond this limit. *Humiliter quantum potest* the theologian, in order to remain a theologian, will *quaerere rationem*

---

[1] *Palam namque est quia illi non habent fidei firmitatem, qui quoniam quod credunt intelligere non possunt, disputant contra eiusdem fidei a sanctis patribus confirmatam veritatem. Velut si vespertiliones et noctuae non nisi in nocte caelum videntes de meridianis solis radiis discepten*t *contra aquilas ipsum solem irreverberato visu intuentes* (*Ep. de incarn. 1:* II 8, 1ff). *Ab iis, qui se Christiani nominis honore gaudere fatentur, iuste exigendum est, ut cautionem in baptismate factam inconcusse teneant* (*Ep. 136:* III 280, 35ff). *Nullus quippe Christianus debet disputare quomodo, quod catholica ecclesia corde credit et ore confitetur, non sit, sed semper eandem fidem indubitanter tenendo, amando et secundum illam vivendo humiliter quantum potest quaerere rationem quomodo sit. Si potest intelligere, Deo gratias agat; si non potest, non immitat cornua ad ventilandum, sed submittat caput ad venerandum* (Ezek. 34.21). *Citius enim potest in se confidens humana sapientia impingendo cornua sibi evellere quam innitendo petram hanc evolvere* (*Ep. de incarn. 1:* II 6, 10–7, 6). In the *prior recensio* of this work Anselm had said: *Deo protegente numquam de hac fide disputabo, quomodo non sit; Deo dante semper credendo, amando, vivendo de illa disputabo, quomodo sit* (I 283, 22ff). *Qui enim pie vivere quaerit, sanctam Scripturam meditatur, et quod nondum intelligit, non reprehendit, quare nec resistit: quod est* (Matt. 5.5) *mitem fieri* (*Hom. 2: MPL* 158, 596).

[2] *Exemplum meditationis de fidei ratione*—is how the original title of the *Monologion* ought to read. *Meditatio parit scientiam* (*Medit. 7, 1: MPL* 158, 741).

quomodo sit. That means that at a certain point he will silence the question *quomodo sit.* Any extension or explication of or meditation upon the acceptance of the *Credo* in faith can be nothing more than a description of this acceptance, that is of the *Credo* accepted. It cannot be—this would be contrary to *humilitas* and we have not the *potestas* to do it—a basis of our acceptance or of the accepted *Credo.* The basis is in the fact of the *Credo* and of the *credo,* in the fact of the divine revelation. The fact itself, as it emerges faintly through the dogma of the three-fold unity of God or of the Incarnation, is inconceivable. Therefore, *intelligere* will not go beyond the limit of the inner necessity of the articles of the *Credo,* beyond the limit of faith's essential nature which corresponds to these articles.[1] The task of theology at this limit—arising from the conception of God that Christianity gives—will rather be *rationabiliter comprehendere incomprehensibile esse, quomodo . . . ;*[2] that is, to consider alongside its demonstration of the inner necessity of Christian truth its factuality, which is derived from no external necessity, and to understand this factuality as the impetus of its inner necessity. Anyone who wants to ask more questions at this limit can only be a fool who, though he hears the revealed Word and has it *in intellectu,* yet because the *res,* the fact of revelation, escapes him, still asks for an external necessity, a *quomodo,* which he can find only in the inner necessity, in the *esse,* of the truth itself which is being proclaimed and which he is calling in question.[3]

---

[1] On the Trinity: *Videtur mihi huius tam sublimis rei secretum transcendere omnem intellectus aciem humani, et idcirco conatum explicandi qualiter hoc sit, continendum puto. Sufficere namque debere existimo rem incomprehensibilem indaganti, si ad hoc ratiocinando pervenerit, ut eam certissime esse cognoscat, etiamsi penetrare nequeat intellectu, quomodo ita sit, nec idcirco minus iis adhibendam fidei certitudinem, quae probationibus necessariis nulla alia repugnante ratione asseruntur, si suae naturalis altitudinis incomprehensibilitate explicari non patiantur* (*Monol. 64:* I 74, 30-75, 6).

On the Incarnation: *Qua vero ratione sapientia Dei hoc fecit, si non possumus intelligere, non debemus mirari, sed cum veneratione tolerare aliquid esse in secretis tantae rei, quod ignoremus* (*C.D.h. II 16:* II 117, 3ff).

[2] *Monol. 64* (I 75, 11f); cf. *Prosl. 15* (I 112, 14ff).

[3] *Quid respondendum est illi, qui idcirco astruit esse impossibile quod necesse est esse, quia nescit, quomodo sit?* Answer: *Quia insipiens est!* . . . *Quod necessaria ratione veraciter esse colligitur, id in nullam deduci debet dubitationem, etiam si ratio, quomodo sit, non percipitur* (*C.D.h. I 25:* II 95, 18ff; 96, 2f).

3. Every theological statement is an inadequate expression of its object.[1] The actual Word of Christ spoken to us is not an inadequate expression of its object,[2] though of course every attempt on our part, even the highest and the best, to reproduce that Word in thought or in speech is inadequate.[3] Strictly speaking, it is only God himself who has a conception of God. All that we have are conceptions of objects, none of which is identical with God. Even the most worthy descriptions are only relatively worthy of him. He is all that we are able to say about him and is not only wholly-other, though certainly he alone is true and real,[4] unique[5] and in a category all his own and known only to himself. Therefore, every one of the categories known to us by which we attempt to conceive him is, in the last analysis, not really one of his categories at all. God shatters every syllogism.[6] But just as everything which is not God could not exist apart from God and is something only because of God, with increasing intensity an *aliqua imitatio illius essentiae*,[7] so it is possible for expressions which are really appropriate only to objects that are not identical with God, to be true expressions, *per aliquam similitudinem aut imaginem (ut cum vultum alicuius consideramus in speculo)*, even when these expressions are

---

[1] *Valde minus aliquid, immo longe aliud in mente mea sua significatione constituunt, quam sit illud, ad quod intelligendum per hanc tenuem significationem mens ipsa mea conatur proficere (Monol. 65: I 76, 27ff).*

[2] *Satis itaque manifestum est in verbo, per quod facta sunt omnia, non esse ipsorum similitudinem, sed veram simplicemque essentiam (Monol. 31: I 50, 7ff).*

[3] *Non tento, Domine, penetrare altitudinem tuam, quia nullatenus comparo illi intellectum meum (Prosl. 1: I 100, 15f).*

[4] *Monol. 28:* I 45, 25ff.

[5] In the uniqueness of the solely, originally Existent One (*Prosl. 22:* I 116, 15ff; *De casu diab. 1:* I 233, 16ff).

[6] *Si quando illi est cum aliis nominis alicuius communio, valde procul dubio intelligenda est diversa significatio (Monol. 26:* I 44, 17ff). *Illa substantia nullo communi substantiarum tractatu includitur (Monol. 27:* I 45, 4f). *Sic est summa essentia supra et extra omnem aliam naturam, ut, si quando de illa dicitur aliquid verbis, quae communia sunt aliis naturis, sensus nullatenus sit communis . . . Quaecumque nomina de illa natura dici posse videntur* (even the *nomina sapienta* and *essentia*) *non tam mihi eam ostendunt per proprietatem . . .* (*Monol. 65:* I 76, 2ff, 22f).

[7] *Monol. 31* and *34, De casu diab. 1.*

applied to the God who can never be expressed.[1] Not all 'speculative' theology says what is true. But even theology which does say what is true is still 'speculative' theology.[2] Theology can neither avoid nor ignore the fact of being thus conditioned; nor ought this to make it ashamed.

4. It follows from this that theological statements can be made with only scientific certainty, which, on account of its relativity, has to be distinguished from the certainty of faith. Theological statements as such are contested statements— challenged by the sheer incomparability of their object.[3] It is just this very absoluteness of the revelation to which his statements apply that isolates the theologian in his meditation, as one who can think about himself with only the relative power of the *ratio certitudinis*,[4] who often will be able to work only by experiment,[5] who waits on the correction of others,[6] who can never assume the ultimate certainty of even his best conceived statements,[7] who will always understand his most profound *intelligere* as nothing more than an *aliquatenus intelligere veritatem tuam*[8] and his science as no more than *imbecillitas scientae meae*.[9] There is one, and only one, apparent exception to this rule: the theologian speaks absolutely when his statements coincide with the text, or with the necessary inferences

---

[1] *Falsum non est, si quid de illa ratione docente per aliud velut in aenigmate potest aestimari* (*Monol. 65:* I 77, 2f).

[2] *Quod speculor* is Anselm's own description of his action (*Monol. 6:* I 19, 19).

[3] *Sic quippe unam eandemque rem dicimus et non dicimus, videmus, et non videmus . . . per aliud;* but not *per suam proprietam* (*Monol. 65:* I 76, 16ff).

[4] *Non potest intellectus meus ad illam. Nimis fulget, non capit illam, nec suffert oculus animae meae diu intendere in illam. Reverberatur fulgore, vincitur amplitudine, obruitur immensitate, confunditur capacitate. O summa et inacessibilis lux! O tota et beata veritas, quam longe es a me, qui tam prope tibi sum! Quam remota es a conspectu meo, qui sic praesens sum conspectui tuo* (*Prosl. 16:* I 112, 24ff).

[5] *Tentabo pro mea possibilitate Deo adiuvante . . .* (*C.D.h. I 2:* II 50, 4). *Si aliquatenus potero, quod postulas ostendere, gratias agamus Deo. Si vero non potero, sufficiant ea, quae supra probata sunt* (*ibid. II 16:* II 117, 23ff).

[6] *Si quid diximus, quod corrigendum sit, non renuo correctionem, si rationabiliter fit* (*ibid. II 22:* II 133, 12f).

[7] *Haec breviter . . . pro capacitate intellectus mei, non tam affirmando quam coniectando dixi, donec mihi Deus melius aliquo modo revelet* (*De conc. virg. 29:* II 173, 4ff).

[8] *Prosl. 1:* I 100, 17.   [9] *C.D.h. I 25:* II 96, 17.

from the text, of the sacred authority.[1] But, as we shall find Anselm explaining later, the task of theology, the quest for *intelligere* in the narrower sense, begins at the very place where biblical quotation stops. Thus, any statement that is really theological, that is to say not covered by biblical authority, is bound by this rule: such a statement is not final; fundamentally it is an interim-statement, the best that knowledge and conscience can for the present construe; it awaits better instruction from God or man.[2]

5. Fundamentally it is possible and indeed necessary for the science of theology to advance along its entire front. Even of the Church Fathers, whom he still regarded as authoritative, Anselm expressly said that we can and must progress beyond the results of their work. In matters of faith-knowledge they have performed a great service, a service in fact which in its own way cannot be surpassed. But on the other hand their life, like all human life, was short and it would be going too far to assume that their writings represent the final achievement of *intelligere* possible to the objective *ratio veritatis* in its relation to human powers of understanding or that further development should be denied us; it is also certain that the Lord who has promised to be with the Church until the end of the world will not cease to pour out the gifts of his grace in her midst.[3] Clearly, in Anselm's mind all this was true not just of the

[1] That this is what Anselm meant follows from his statement that the theologian does not speak absolutely without the express mandate of the biblical authority (*Monol. 1:* I 14, 1ff; *C.D.h. I 2:* II 50, 7ff; *ibid. 18:* II 82, 5ff; *De proc. Spir. 11:* II 209, 14).

[2] *Non alia certudine accipiatur, nisi quia interim ita mihi videtur, donec Deus mihi melius aliquo modo revelet* (*C.D.h. I 2:* II 50, 9f). *Sic volo accipi ut, quamvis ex rationibus quae mihi videbuntur, quasi necessarium concludatur, non ob hoc tamen omnino necessarium, sed tantum sic interim videri posse dicatur* (*Monol. 1:* I 14, 2ff). *Dicam igitur sic breviter de hoc quod sentio, ut nullius de eadem re fidelem improbem sententiam, nec meam, si veritati repugnare probari rationabiliter poterit pervicaciter defendam* (*De conc. virg. Prologue:* II 139, 10ff).

[3] *Quamvis post apostolos sancti patres et doctores nostri multi tot et tanta de fidei nostrae ratione dicant . . . ut nec nostris nec futuris temporibus ullum illis parem in veritatis contemplatione speremus: nullum tamen reprehendendum arbitror, si fide stabilitus in rationis eius indagine se voluerit exercere. Nam et illi, quia breves dies hominis sunt* (Job 14.5), *non omnia quae possent, si diutius vixissent, dicere potuerunt; et veritatis ratio tam ampla tamque profunda est, ut a mortalibus nequeat exhauriri; et Dominus in ecclesia sua, cum qua se esse usque ad consummationem saeculi promittit, gratiae suae dona non desinit impertiri* (*C.D.h. comm. op.:* II 39, 2-40, 7).

theology of the Church Fathers but of all theology. He is aware not only of the existence of those *maiores et plures rationes* of truth which must remain ultimately closed to the human spirit ('ultimately' at least as far as this world is concerned),[1] but he is also aware of the existence of *rationes* which for the present are hidden but are intrinsically accessible and have still to be laid bare in the future.[2] We are therefore justified in ascribing to Anselm the explicit notion of progress in theology, in so far as he thought of the scientific process as an ascent from one *ratio* to an ever higher *ratio*.[3] In this connection it should, however, be noted that this progress which takes place from time to time at particular moments of history is not at the mercy of the theologian's whim but is conditioned by the wisdom of God who well knows what it is good for us to perceive at any given time.[4] That the perfectibility of theology implies for Anselm both stop[5] and start must not be ignored.

6. We have, however, one concrete criterion for all theological statements, though not the kind of criterion that enables us to value such statements positively, that is assess their specific value as knowledge. This verdict, the verdict whether a particular scientific contribution is really *intelligere*, that is whether it signifies progress in *intelligere*, rests in a provisional sense with the author, his readers, those with whom he carries on the debate and those who listen to it.[6] But of course in the ultimate sense it is hidden and remains hidden with God who himself is Truth. The fundamental reason for the vulnerability

---

[1] *C.D.h. I 2:* II 50, 12; *ibid. II 19:* II 131, 14f.

[2] *C.D.h. I 2:* II 50, 8ff; *De conc. virg. 21:* II 161, 3ff.

[3] *Debes . . . sperare de gratia Dei, quia si ea quae gratis accepisti libenter impertiris, altiora, ad quae nondum attigisti, mereberis accipere* (*C.D.h. I 1:* II 49, 3ff). It is worth noting that Anselm gives this thought a specially prominent position in that very first chapter of *Cur Deus homo*, where his scientific self-consciousness has perhaps reached its peak.

[4] *Da mihi, ut, quantum scis expedire, intelligam* (*Prosl. 2:* I 101, 3f).

[5] *Si aliquatenus quaestioni tuae satisfacere potero, certum esse debebit, quia et sapientior me plenius hoc facere poterit. Immo sciendum est, quidquid inde homo dicere possit, altiores tantae rei adhuc latere rationes* (*C.D.h. I 2:* II 50, 10ff).

[6] Under this category come the more or less favourable conclusions with which, for example in the *Cur Deus homo*, Boso (or Anselm by the mouth of Boso) usually underlines the completion of individual trains of thought.

of theology that follows from the inadequacy, the merely scientific certainty and the perfectibility of its language, is this —while the best of its statements can find human approval, it is not possible for the final criterion of this approval to be demonstrated or appealed to. There is, however, one criterion which at least determines whether a theologoumenon is admissible or not. This criterion is the text of Holy Scripture, which according to Anselm forms the basic stability of the *Credo* to which the *credere* and therefore the *intelligere* refer. While it is the decisive source, it is also the determining norm of *intelligere*, the *auctoritas veritatis, quam ratio colligit*.[1] In this respect Anselm's rule runs as follows: If a proposition accords with the actual wording of the Bible or with the direct inferences from it, then naturally it is valid with absolute certainty, but just because of this agreement it is not strictly a theological proposition. If, on the other hand, it is a strictly theological proposition, that is to say a proposition formed independently of the actual wording of Scripture, then the fact that it does not contradict the biblical text, determines its validity. But if it did contradict the Bible, however attractive it might be on other grounds, it would be rendered invalid.[2]

7. A further condition of *intelligere*, however, is the reality of *credere* in and for itself. It is also absolutely decisive for knowledge that what is Right should be rightly believed. But right belief is simply belief that is a human act of response and that is by definition a *tendere in Deum. Illam credere nisi tendat in illam,*

---

[1] *De concordia Qu. III 6:* II 272, 6f. It will be noticed that Boso, the opponent in the discussion in *Cur Deus homo*, (for example, as in *I 3:* II 50, 20ff), does not by any means represent only doubt with his questions but, in drawing attention to apparently contradictory biblical passages, he represents the ecclesiastical authority as well. Theological science has also to justify itself on this score.

[2] *Nam si quid ratione dicimus aliquando, quod in dictis eius (sc. sacrae scripturae) aperte monstrare aut ex ipsis probare nequimus: hoc modo per illam cognoscimus utrum sit accipiendum aut respuendum. Si enim aperta ratione colligitur et illa ex nulla parte contradicit (quoniam ipsa sicut nulli adversatur veritati, ita nulli favet falsitati): hoc ipso, quia non negat quod ratione dicitur, eius auctoritate suscipitur. At, si ipsa nostro sensui indubitanter repugnat, quamvis nobis ratio nostra videatur inexpugnabilis, nulla tamen veritate fulciri credenda est (De concordia Qu. III 6:* II 271, 28-272, 6). *Certus enim sum, si quid dico quod sacrae scripturae absque dubio contradicat, quia falsum est; nec illud tenere volo, si cognovero (C.D.h. I 18:* II 82, 8ff).

nulli prodest.[1] Faith does not mean only *credere id*, but also *credere in id, quod credi debet*, otherwise for all its supposed certainty it is a faith that is useless and dead.[2] Are faith and the knowledge of faith based on the Word of God? Most certainly; but when we speak of the gift of this Word, the effect of the Word is, invariably, that both the Word and the event of hearing the Word are understood together.[3] Are faith and the knowledge of faith matters of the heart? Most certainly; but for that very reason also matters of the will—for how could there be a right heart where right faith and right knowledge of faith are not willed?[4] Now where this right faith is absent there can be no right knowledge; in that case the scientific nature of theology is called in question just as much as when the thing believed is false.[5] Anselm saw these two fatal difficulties in the closest relation. For that reason he could not emphasize too strongly (in his warning against the theology of bats and owls) that prior to any desire or ability to find theological answers is the question of dedication on the part of the theologian himself. What is required is a pure heart, eyes that have been opened, child-like obedience, a life in the Spirit, rich nourishment from Holy Scripture to make him capable of finding these answers.[6] For him it goes without saying that

---

[1] *Monol. 77:* I 84, 12f.   [2] *Monol. 78:* I 85, 8f; *De concordia Qu. III 2:* II 265, 10f.

[3] *Est autem semen huius agriculturae verbum Dei, immo non verbum, sed sensus qui percipitur per verbum. Vox namque sine sensu nihil constituit in corde (De concordia Qu. III 6:* II 270, 23ff).

[4] *Quamvis enim corde credamus et intelligamus, sicut corde volumus, non tamen iudicat Spiritus sanctus illum rectum habere cor, qui recte credit et intelligit et non recte vult; quia non utitur rectitudine fidei et intellectus ad recte volendum, propter quod datum est rationali creaturae recte credere et intelligere (ibid. Qu. III 2:* II 265, 5ff). *Addita namque rectitudine volendi conceptioni per gratiam fit fides (ibid. Qu. III 6:* II 271, 8f).

[5] *Neque rectum intellectum habere dicendus est, qui secundum illum non recte vult (ibid. Qu. III 2:* II 265, 9f). *Non solum ad intelligendum altiora prohibetur mens ascendere sine fide et mandatorum Dei oboedientia sed etiam aliquando datus intellectus subtrahitur . . . neglecta bona conscientia (Ep. de incarn. 1:* II 9, 9ff).

[6] *Prius ergo fide mundandum est cor . . . et prius per praeceptorum Domini custodiam illuminandi sunt oculi . . . et prius per humilem oboedientiam testimoniorum Dei debemus fieri parvuli. . . . Prius inquam ea quae carnis sunt postponentes secundum spiritum vivamus quam profunda fidei diiudicando discutiamus. . . . Verum enim est quia quanto opulentius nutrimur in sacra scriptura ex iis, quae per oboedientiam pascunt, tanto subtilius provehimur ad ea, quae per intellectum satiant (Ep. de incarn. 1:* II 8, 7ff).

where faith is really faith, that is to say obedience, the fight between bats and owls over the reality of the sun's rays will just not happen and that a theology that is grounded on the obedience of faith will be a positive theology. He knows perfectly well that in saying this he is taking a risk and so he adds that even this necessary connection between faith in what is right and right faith (and *vice versa*) has to be taken in faith to be understood. For only in faith could this connection between the obedience of faith and the faith of the Church be experienced and only in experience could it be understood.[1] Thus it cannot be denied that, faced with the danger on the one hand of a dead orthodoxy and on the other of a flightiness that is only too much alive, Anselm here applied a similar corrective[2] to that applied later by Melancthon with his demand for a fiducial faith or still later by Pietism with its emphasis on the experience of rebirth or by present-day theologians in their demand for 'existential' thinking. However, it is most instructive to see how very conscious Anselm himself obviously was of the provisional nature of this condition of *intelligere*. Though it means for him one of many serious questions, it is not the final question.

8. When we consider the connection which Anselm held to be necessary between theology and prayer we put our finger on the condition of *intelligere* which, unless we are completely mistaken, emerges at this point as *sui generis* from all the others and which conditions all these others and makes them relative.[3]

---

[1] *Nimirum hoc ipsum quod dico: qui non crediderit, non intelliget. Nam qui non crediderit, non experietur: et qui expertus non fuerit, non cognoscet (ibid. 1: II 9, 5f)*—this sentence, as is well known, appears alongside *Credo ut intelligam* on the title page of Schliermacher's *Glaubenslehre* and speaks of the 'experience' of the necessity that right personal obedience of faith should be related to the faith of the Church and it claims that faith is superior to this experience.

[2] *Nemo ergo se temere immergat in condensa divinarum quaestionum, nisi prius in soliditate fidei conquisita morum et sapientiae gravitate, ne per multiplicia sophismatum diverticula incauta levitate discurrens, aliqua tenaci illaqueetur falsitate (ibid. 1: II 9, 16ff).*

[3] Including particularly the last-mentioned, the authenticity of *credere*. On one occasion, praying for the illuminating grace of God, Anselm thankfully (if that be overlooked the whole passage cannot but be misunderstood) dares the bold statement that now he has clearly recognized that this knowledge would still

When his *Monologion* lay finished before him Anselm felt compelled to work through for a second time what was essentially the same material—the doctrine of God in the narrower sense—in the form of the *Proslogion*, that is, in the form of an explicit address to God. But even this form did not become his literary pattern. In *Cur Deus homo* and other writings we see him make use of the dialogue form between teacher and student. In *De concordia*, one of his later works, a tendency can be noted towards the method of the *Quaestiones*, which became characteristic of later Scholasticism. And all his life in the *Meditationes* he developed, as an alternative to the invocation form of the *Proslogion*, the monologue of the soul on the things of God and man. For this reason it must not be overlooked that in the form of the *Proslogion* an attitude manifests itself whose significance for his whole inquiry transcends matters of style and indeed things human.[1] It is in *Cur Deus homo*, technically perhaps Anselm's most complete work, that indications of this attitude keep breaking through. He is to expound *quod Deus mihi dignabitur aperire*.[2] He reminds his colleague of the duty that his questions impose of interceding for the teacher.[3] Boso interrupts at one of the great highlights in the exposition of the Proof with an adoring, '*Benedictus Deus*'.[4] And when at another point he expresses amazement at the masterly conduct of the discussion, Anselm's reply is that guidance along the path of

remain to him even were he to refuse to believe: *Gratias tibi, bone Domine, gratias tibi; quia quod prius credidi, te donante, iam sic intelligo, te illuminante, ut, si te esse nolim credere, non possim non intelligere (Prosl. 4:* I 104, 5ff).

[1] 'We are well able to listen to the enchanted language of such passages now that the Enlightenment has been disposed of by Herder, Classicism and Romanticism. But even today this kind of thing is taken as a purely subjective result of feeling, whereas that of logical succession is taken as an entirely objective product of the intellect and so any real understanding of either is prevented by this wedge that is driven between them right at the start'—this objection of W. von den Steinen (*Vom Heiligen Geist des Mittelalters*, 1926, pp. 36f) is only too true.

[2] *C.D.h. I I:* II 48, 10.

[3] *Deo adiuvante et vestris orationibus, quas hoc postulantes saepe mihi petenti ad hoc ipsum promisistis (ibid. I 2:* II 50, 4ff).

[4] . . . *iam magnum quiddam invenimus de hoc quod quaerimus. Prosequere igitur, ut incepisti. Spero enim, quia Deus nos adiuvabit (ibid. II 6:* II 101, 20f).

truth must have been God's doing.[1] To this the closing words
of the book correspond: *Si autem veritatis testimonio roboratur,
quod nos rationabiliter invenisse existimamus, Deo non nobis attribuere
debemus, qui est benedictus in saecula. Amen.*[2] There is more in this
than just the general, though of course true, statement that for
Anselm right knowledge is conditioned by the prevenient and
co-operating grace of God.[3] This general consideration and also
the fact that this grace must ever be sought by prayer already
imply that the ultimate and decisive capacity for the *intellectus
fidei* does not belong to human reason acting on its own but
has always to be bestowed[4] on human reason as surely as
intelligere is a *voluntarius effectus*.[5] It is also true that this capacity
which is bestowed consists in following correctly the successive
logical steps that lead to knowledge. The *donum gratiae*, the
subject of Anselm's prayer, is from this point of view identical
with seeking and attaining the highest reach of human thinking.[6] But that, however, is just one side of the matter. A
careful reading of the relevant text of the opening prayer of the
Proslogion[7] shows that all the way through what Anselm has in
mind as the object of his request is twofold. The first of course
is—that God would instruct his heart, *ubi et quomodo te
quaerat*, that God would enlighten his eyes, that he who by
nature ever stoops to earth might be lifted up to look on him.
Here we cannot fail to recognize this aspect of grace as the
actualization of that power to know which was originally

---

[1] *Non ego te duco, sed ille, de quo loquimur, sine quo nihil possumus, nos ducit ubicumque viam veritatis tenemus (ibid. II 9:* II 106, 7f).

[2] *Ibid. II 22:* II 133, 13ff. *Si qui dixi, quod quaerenti cuilibet sufficere debeat, non mihi imputo, quia non ego sed gratia Dei mecum (De concordia Qu. III 14:* II 288, 12ff).

[3] Knowledge belongs to the *dona gratiae* which the Lord of the Church never ceases to pour out upon her (*C.D.h. comm. op.:* II 40, 6). *Et praedicatio est gratia . . . et auditus est gratia et intellectus ex auditu gratia et rectitudo volendi gratia est (De concordia Qu. III 6:* II 271, 11ff).

[4] *Ergo Domine, qui das fidei intellectum, da mihi, ut . . . intelligam (Prosl. 2:* I 101, 3). *Revela me de me ad te (Prosl. 18:* I 114, 10f).

[5] *Monol. 68:* I 78, 16.

[6] *Munda, sana, acue, illumina oculum mentis meae, ut intueatur te (Prosl. 18:* I 114, 11f).

[7] *Prosl. 1:* I 97ff.

created in man. But the occurrence of *intellectus* and therefore the requested grace has still another objective aspect. Anselm places alongside this request a second—it seems to me impossible to take it as a mere rhetorical repetition of the first in view of the whole tenor of the context—that God would instruct his heart. *ubi et quomodo te inveniat,* that God would let him see his face, let him see his very Self.[1] That God would give himself to him again. He interprets the plight of man in his failure to know God, a plight which even the believer shares,[2] as being due to the fact that he is involved in the remoteness from God of a humanity that is sinful by inheritance.[3] This remoteness is clearly an objective remoteness of God himself— God is absent, he dwells in light unapproachable. What is the man who yearns for him to do? *Anhelat videre te et nimis abest illi facies tua; accedere ad te desiderat et inaccessibilis est habitatio tua . . . Usquequo Domine oblivisceris nos, usquequo avertis faciem tuam a nobis? Quando respicies et exaudies nos . . . et ostendes nobis faciem tuam?* Both then mean: *Nec quaerete re possum, nisi tu doceas, nec invenire, nisi te ostendas.* What is at stake here is not just the right way to seek God, but in addition God's presence, on which the whole grace of Christian knowledge primarily depends, the encounter with him which can never be brought about by all our searching for God however thorough it may be, although it is only to the man who seeks God with a pure heart that this encounter comes. We are already acquainted to some extent with the dialectic in the concept *intelligere.*[4] That there is also an *intelligere esse in re* only *aliquatenus* is not self-evident. Even this modified *intelligere* by which man is enabled to see something of the very face of God, has to be sought in prayer for all right seeking (it also is grace) would be of no avail if God did not 'show' himself, if the encounter with him were not in fact

---

[1] *Ostende nobis teipsum (ibid.:* I 99, 18f).

[2] *Tu me fecisti et refecisti, et omnia mea bona tu mihi contulisti, et nondum novi te (ibid.:* I 98, 13f).

[3] *Heu me miserum, unum de aliis miseris filiis Evae, elongatis a Deo (ibid.:* I 99, 8).

[4] Cf. pp. 24f.

primarily a movement from his side and if the finding that goes with it, the modified *intelligere*, did not take place. It is only from this point of view that the attitude of Anselm which is becoming obvious in the *Proslogion* can be fully understood. This attitude is not just that of a 'pious' thinker who offers his work to the service of the divine work that his work may be done well. It is that of course. But above and beyond that[1] it is a specific and perhaps the most decisive expression of his scientific objectivity. Everything depends not only on the fact that God grants him grace to think correctly about him, but also on the fact that God himself comes within his system as the object of this thinking, that he 'shows' himself to the thinker and in so doing modifies 'correct' thinking to an *intelligere esse in re*. Only thus does the grace of Christian knowledge become complete. The author of the *Proslogion* keeps up the address to God on which he has embarked, not in order to extort this fulness of grace, but because he knows this fulness of grace to be essential. In this attitude he stands in encounter with God for he knows that God must stand in encounter with him if his *intelligere* is not to be delusion and if he himself is not to be a mere *insipiens*. The Proof, *Prosl. 2-4*, is also conducted in this attitude and in this knowledge. We cannot be indifferent to this if we are to understand and interpret him.[2]

To summarize what has been established: The knowledge, the *intellectus*, with which Anselm is concerned is the *intellectus fidei*. That means that it can consist only of positive meditation on the object of faith. It cannot establish this object of faith as

---

[1] *Auge desiderium meum et da quod peto, quoniam si cuncta quae fecisti, mihi dederis, non sufficit servo tuo, nisi teipsum dederis. Da ergo teipsum mihi, Deus meus, redde te mihi* (*Medit. 14, 2: MPL* 158, 781).

[2] With sure instinct Kierkegaard found here the thing that interests him in Anselm's Proof of the Existence of God: 'Moreover, his own way—of proving. Anselm says, "I want to prove the existence of God. To that end I ask God to strengthen and help me"—but that is surely a much better proof of the existence of God, namely, the certainty that to prove it we need God's help. If we were able to prove the existence of God without his help, that would be as if it were less certain that he is there. . . .' (Walter Ruttenbeck, *Sören Kierkegaard*, 1930, p. 143).

such but rather has to understand it in its very incomprehensibility. Yet nevertheless, it has to progress at the level of reflection, expressing in symbols what in itself cannot be expressed. It will therefore be able to claim only scientific certainty for its results and not the certainty of faith and it will therefore not deny the fundamental imperfection of these results. It will not on any account be able to set itself in explicit contradiction to the Bible, the textual basis of the revealed object of faith. And it would not be what it is or achieve what it does achieve if it were not the knowledge of faith-obedience. In the end, the fact that it reaches its goal is grace, both with regard to the perception of the goal and the human effort to reach it; and therefore in the last analysis it is a question of prayer and the answer to prayer.

4. THE MANNER OF THEOLOGY

Having defined our terms, it ought to be a comparatively simple matter to show the type of function that Anselm understood the *intellectus* to have.

In explaining Anselm's use of '*intelligere*' it is vitally important to remember the literal meaning of the word: *intus legere*. After all that we have said there can be no question but that the fundamental meaning of *intelligere* in Anselm is *legere*: to reflect upon what has already been said in the *Credo*. In recognizing and assenting to truth *intelligere* and *credere* come together and the *intelligere* is itself and remains a *credere* while the *credere* in and by itself, as we have seen, is also an embryonic *intelligere*. But *intelligere* means still more than that: to read and ponder what has been already said—that is to say, in the appropriation of truth, actually to traverse that intervening distance (between recognition and assent) and so therefore to understand the truth as truth. Corresponding to the position of post-Adamic man, as we have just heard from *Prosl. 1*, the *credere* and this real *intelligere* are to be distinguished not just abstractly but also in practice, for they do not coincide in the sense that the believer simply possesses or can automatically acquire the *intellectus fidei*, the understanding of the *Credo* by his own thought. Rather he must seek it in prayer and by the persistent application of his intellectual powers. He will not seek it anywhere outside of or apart from the revealed *Credo* of the Church and certainly not apart from or outside of Holy Scripture. Anselm is distinguished from the 'liberal' theologians of his time in that his *intelligere* is really intended to be no more than a deepened form of *legere*. But—and this distinguishes him just as definitely from the 'positivists', the traditionalists of his day—it does involve a deepened *legere*, an *intus legere*, a reflecting upon. So as sons and heirs of Adam we are not confronted by the truth revealed in Scripture in such a way that, when the hearing or reading of the outward text is crowned by faith (certain as it is that this text is the full revealed truth), we are then absolved from the task of understanding it as truth, which, though divinely given, has still to be sought by human means. From our point of view, the revealed truth has, as it were, an inner text which of course simply asserts that what to us is the outward text is the truth, according to its claim to authority and to our faith. This inner text can be found only within the outward text, but cannot simply be heard or read along with the outward text, for it can be sought and found in the outward text only by virtue of a distinct intention and act and also—and this is decisive—only by virtue of special grace. Scripture is of course *super solidam veritatem . . . velut super firmum fundamentum fundata*. And this its 'basis' is clear to us in faith. But even though it is all that, it is still a problem for our understanding and we are confronted with the task of examining the thing itself that is revealed and believed—within the limits of this 'itself' and therefore it can be only 'to some extent', *Deo adiuvante aliquatenus perspicere veritatem*.[1] Not only objective truth as such, but its inner meaning, its basis and its

[1] *C.D.h. II 19:* II 131, 9f.

context, as we discern them, ought to bear witness that what Scripture declares is in fact so.[1]

Consequently it cannot be—if it is to be *perspicere* too—that *intelligere* consists in our bringing to remembrance a text of Scripture which confirms the contents of an article of faith in order to establish that article of faith. That would be to revert to the obviously indispensable presupposition of *intelligere*, to the believing *legere*.[2] The opposition and derision of unbelievers and the uncertainty even of believing Christians, the questions of the wise and the foolish over the text of Scripture and the *Credo*[3] all show that humanly speaking the inner and the outward text of the revelation are by no means a unity; that their meaning, basis and context, and with these their truth, are not such that we can simply read them off, but on the contrary for us they are wrapped in mystery and we can grasp them only by a special effort of understanding that goes beyond mere reading. It is true that the Word appropriated in faith is also in itself, as a mere *vox significans rem in intellectu*, the whole saving truth full of meaning and with its own basis and context. But it is precisely as such that we are intended to grasp it.[4] So the recital of 'proof-texts' as confirmation would do no more than state the problem all over again and would contribute nothing to its solution. This is asserted by the methodological principle which Anselm strongly emphasized—that when it is a question of *intelligere* and *probare* nothing can be achieved by an appeal to the authority of Holy

---

[1] *Quatenus . . . quidquid per singulas investigationes finis assereret id ita esse . . . et rationis necessitas breviter cogeret et veritatis claritas patenter ostenderet (Monol. Prologue:* I 7, 7ff). *Monstratur. . . . ratione et veritate (C.D.h. Preface:* II 42, 14f).

[2] As a theologian Anselm will *non tam ostendere, quam tecum quaerere (C.D.h. I 2:* II 50, 6).

[3] *Quam quaestionem solent et infideles nobis simplicitatem Christianam quasi fatuam deridentes obicere, et fideles multi in corde versare . . . De qua quaestione non solum litterati, sed etiam illitterati multi quaerunt et rationem eius desiderant (C.D.h. I 1:* II 47, 11-48, 6).

[4] *Quapropter summo studio animum ad hoc intenderat, quatenus iuxta fidem suam mentis ratione mereretur percipere, quae in ipsis (sc. scripturis) sensit multa caligine tecta latere (Vita S. Anselmi auctore Eadmero, lib. I cap. 2 §9: MPL* 158, 55).

Scripture.[1] The much disputed rule which Anselm adopted for his work *Cur Deus homo* is no more than a special application of this principle—that the discussion of Christology is to be argued *remoto Christo, quasi numquam aliquid fuerit de illo . . . quasi nihil sciatur de Christo*.[2] All this does not mean that it was Anselm's intention to suspend Holy Scripture completely as source and norm of his thinking so as to reconstruct the *Credo* apart from the contents of Scripture, *tabula rasa*, from elements of knowledge obtained elsewhere. The commentary on this passage which is often overlooked and yet which is our best guide bears testimony to what Anselm has actually done in *Cur Deus homo*, as in all his other works. It is abundantly clear from this that not for a moment do Scripture and *Credo* cease to be the presupposition and object of his thinking, only that whenever he comes up against a particular problem where he is concerned with its scientific answer, he refrains from drawing upon the statements of the Bible or the *Credo* for his answer or basing his answer upon their authority. That is to say, he refrains from introducing or quoting 'it is written' as a substitute for scientific investigation (the nature of which we have still to discuss), at a point where it is the very quotation that requires to be considered and understood.[3]

It is mainly from this standpoint that another much disputed methodological formula of Anselm's is to be understood. He says: In all enquiries[4] and demonstrations[5] the rule *sole ratione*

---

[1] *Quatenus auctoritate scripturae penitus nihil in ea (sc. meditatione) persuaderetur* (*Monol. Prologue:* I 7, 7f). *Huic homini non est respondendum auctoritate sacrae scripturae, quia aut ei non credit, aut eam perverso sensu interpretatur* (*Ep. de incarn. 2:* II 11, 5f). *Ut, quod fide tenemus . . . sine scripturae auctoritate probari possit* (*ibid. 6:* II 20, 18f).

[2] *C.D.h. Preface:* II 42, 12ff. *Ponamus . . . incarnationem . . . numquam fuisse (ibid. I 10:* II 67, 12f). *Christum et Christianam fidem quasi numquam fuisset posuimus (ibid. I 20:* II 88, 4f). *Quasi de illo, qui numquam fuerit (ibid. II 10:* II 106, 20). *Ante experimentum. . . . (ibid. II 11:* II 111, 28).

[3] The statement of the Roman Breviary (21 April, *Lectio* 6) that at the Council of Bari (1098) Anselm defended the Latin doctrine of the outpouring of the Holy Spirit *innumeris scripturarum et sanctorum patrum testimoniis*, corresponds neither to his normal procedure nor to the contents of his special essay on that question. On the contrary, Anselm is in fact the exponent of a method of theological exposition that almost completely dispenses with supporting quotations.

[4] *C.D.h. I 20:* II 88, 8.   [5] *C.D.h. II 11:* II 111, 28.

should be kept[1] so as to satisfy Jews and even Gentiles in disputation.[2] This formula, which as we have explained precludes collision with authority, is as liable to be understood or misunderstood as was Luther's *sola fide* in its context. It cannot be understood as if Anselm had written *solitaria ratione*. Authority is the necessary presupposition of Anselm's *ratio*, just as works are the necessary consequence of Luther's *fides*. But just as, for Luther, *fides* alone can justify, so for Anselm *ratio* alone is to be accepted as the suitable criterion in the service of *intelligere* in its narrower, stricter sense.

But what does *ratio* mean in Anselm?

Understanding of this decisive concept is immediately complicated by the fact that the word is continually used as much in the ablative as in the accusative and so can obviously denote both the means to as well as the end of his 'seeking'. If he says *ratione*[3] then *ratio* seems to denote the means to the desired *intellectus*, but if, on the other hand, he speaks of *rationem esurire*,[4] *quaerere*,[5] *ostendere*,[6] *intelligere*,[7] of *meditari de ratione*,[8] then it seems to denote the desired *intellectus* itself. We will be justified in thinking primarily in the first case of man's knowing *ratio* and in the second case of the *ratio* that is to be known, the ratio that belongs to the object of faith itself. 'Primarily'—for when we look at the details of Anselm's remarkable definition of these two *rationes* and their mutual relations we shall have to be prepared for a great deal of overlapping. There is no doubt that Anselm is conscious of something akin to a knowing *ratio* peculiar to man. On one occasion he uses *ratio* to describe the primary capacity of dealing with

---

[1] *Monol. 1:* I 13, 11.   [2] *C.D.h. II 22:* II 133, 8.

[3] Or *mihi ducem rationem sequenti* (*Monol. 29:* I 47, 5) or: *ratione docente* (*Monol. 65:* I 77 3) or: *ratione ducente* (*Monol. 1:* I 13, 15) or: *rationabiliter* (*De proc. Spir. 1:* II 177, 9; *Ep. 136:* III 281, 37; *C.D.h. I 25:* II 96, 7; *ibid. II 22:* II 133, 13; *et al.*), or: *ex rationibus* (*Monol. 1:* I 14, 2) or: *rationibus necessariis* (*Ep. de incarn. 6:* II 20, 19; *C.D.h. Preface:* II 42, 12; *et. al.*).

[4] *C.D.h. comm. op.:* II 39, 5.   [5] *C.D.h. I 3:* II 50, 19.

[6] *C.D.h. I 25:* II 96, 6; *ibid. II 16:* II 116, 17.   [7] *C.D.h. II 16:* II 117, 21.

[8] *Prosl. Prologue:* I 93, 2.

experience, of formulating conceptions and judgments and he calls this: *et princeps, et iudex omnium quae sunt in homine.*[1] And he calls man (along with angels, as distinct from all other creatures)[2] a *rationalis natura* and understands by his rationality the capacity of forming judgments, the capacity of deciding between true and false, good and evil, etc.[3] I know, however, of only one passage in Anselm where the human side of *ratio* is emphasized and therefore its contrast to the objective *ratio* to a certain extent made prominent.[4] But he has clearly gone beyond the idea of human (or even angelic) ability to form concepts or judgments, when he comes to speak of the *ratio quaestionis*[5] or of the *ratio certitudinis meae*[6] or of the *ratio fidei*[7] or of the *ratio* of the words and acts of God, of the *ratio* of their necessity and possibility.[8] The primary result of these various relationships is the conception of a *ratio* peculiar to the object of faith and we can say: if an ontic *ratio* were to be proved by means of the knowing *ratio* of the human faculty of making concepts and judgments, after the object of faith is given by revelation, then this conception would not be correctly interpreted until we take into account that Anselm recognizes a third and ultimate *ratio*, a *ratio veritatis.*[9] Strictly understood the *ratio veritatis* is identical with the *ratio summae naturae*, that is with the divine Word[10] consubstantial with the Father. It is the *ratio* of God.[11] It is not because it is *ratio* that it has truth but because God, Truth, has it. This Word is not divine as word,

---

1 *Ep. de incarn. 1:* II 10, 1f. The passage is directed against the sensuality of the heretical disputers.

2 The realm of spirits, made up of men and angels, if not shared in by the rest of creation also, according to Anselm, is the aim and end of the ways of God and is called the *rationalis et beata civitas* (*C.D.h. I 18:* II 80, 17).

3 *De verit. 12:* I 193, 2; *Monol. 68:* I 78, 21; *C.D.h. I 15:* II 73, 2; *ibid. II 1:* I 97, 4.

4 *Ratio nostra* (*De concordia Qu. III 6:* II 272, 5).   5 *C.D.h. I 1:* II 48, 5.

6 *C.D.h. I 25:* II 96, 7.   7 *Prosl. Prologue:* I 93, 2; *C.D.h. comm. op.:* II 39, 3.

8 *C.D.h. II 15:* II 116, 5f.

9 *C. Gaun. 3:* I 133, 11; *C.D.h. comm. op.:* II 40, 4; *C.D.h. II 19:* II 130, 29; or: *veritatis soliditas rationabilis* (*C.D.h. I 4:* II 52, 3).

10 *Monol. 9f.*   11 *Deus nihil sine ratione facit* (*C.D.h. II 10:* II 108, 23f).

but because it is begotten of the Father—spoken by him. The following holds good only of all those other *rationes* with which the *ratio Dei* is not identical but which as the *ratio* of his creation participate in the *ratio Dei*: Truth is not bound to it but it is bound to Truth.[1] That first of all applies to the noetic *ratio*. In view of his use of the noetic *ratio* Anselm might (I know no instance) also have used the inversion—*veritas rationis*. But in that case the *veritas rationis* would obviously be identical with the *veritas significationis* (with the truth for example of a proposition) and above all it would be subject to the rule that it (when we mean more than the 'truth' of the natural power of thinking and speaking: *ad quod facta est*) absolutely conditioned by the conformity of the *significatio* to the object that is described.[2] In this the correct usage fixed by the object determines whether it is really a *veritas rationis nostrae* that can be meant. But even the truth of the object's existence and nature is dependent not upon itself but upon the divine Word (and so on the real *ratio veritatis* strictly understood) through which it is created. This Word in creating it also confers upon it a resemblance to the truth which belongs to itself (as the Word spoken from God).[3] The way in which the right use of the human *ratio* is determined primarily by its object is therefore, as it were, only the operation by means of which Truth, that is God himself, makes this decision.[4] What is meant by the human *ratio* with regard to truth can therefore in no circum-

---

[1] *Summa veritas per se subsistens nullius rei est, sed cum aliquid secundum illam est, tunc eius dicitur veritas vel rectitudo* (*De verit. 13:* I 199, 27ff). *Nullo claudi potest veritas principio vel fine* (*Monol. 18:* I 33, 21f).

[2] *Oratio . . . cum significat esse quod est* (*cf. non esse quod non est*) *tunc est in ea veritas et est vera* (*De verit. 2:* I 178, 6f).

[3] *Sic existendi veritas intelligatur in verbo, cuius essentia sic summe est, ut quodam modo illa sola sit; in iis vero, quae in eius comparatione quodam modo non sunt et tamen per illud et secundum illud facta sunt aliquid, imitatio aliqua summae illius essentiae perpendatur* (*Monol. 31:* I 49, 3ff).

[4] *Cum veritas, quae est in rerum existentia, sit effectum summae veritatis, ipsa quoque causa est veritatis, quae conitationis est, et eius quae in propositione*, that means 'by the will of' (*De verit. 10:* I 190, 9ff).

46

stances be one that is creative and normative.[1] Secondly, as far as ontic *ratio* is concerned it follows from what has been said, that its part in truth is fundamentally the same but higher than that of the noetic *ratio*: its part like every part of truth itself, as the truth of all *rationes*, has to be conferred. But while this conferring on the side of the noetic *ratio* is a matter of decision that has to be made from time to time, it has to be said about the ontic *ratio* that truth is conferred upon it with the creation of the object of which it is the *ratio*. This is of course specially true of the *ratio fidei* with which Anselm deals. For him, it is without question identical in the proper and strict sense with the *ratio veritatis*. And even here decision enters into it, not as to whether it is *ratio veritatis* but whether it can be recognized as such. In the *Credo* and in the Bible it is hidden and must reveal itself in order to make itself known to us.[2] It does this, however, only if and in so far as the Truth, God himself, does it. Thus: from time to time in the event of knowing, it happens that the noetic *ratio* of the *veritas* conforms to the ontic and to that extent is or is not *vera ratio*—or (and this is normally the case *in praxi*) is to some extent *aliquatenus*. Fundamentally, the *ratio* either as ontic or noetic is never higher than the truth but truth is itself the master of all *rationes* beyond the contrast between ontic and noetic, deciding for itself, now here, now there, what is *vera ratio*: in so far as the *ratio* of the object of faith and the use which man makes of his capacity to think and judge conform to Truth (by virtue of Truth's own decision) its true rationality is determined and the *intellectus* that is sought occurs.

There are a few observations on what has just been said, which must be made at this point before we pursue further the structure of Anselm's conception of *ratio*.

1. We must draw attention to the light that is shed from this unexpected quarter on the relationships already discussed,

[1] *Et istae duae veritates (sc. cogitationis et propositionis) nullius sunt causa veritatis* (*ibid. 10:* I 190, 11f).

[2] Therefore: *ratio veritatis nos docuit* (*C.D.h. II 19:* II 130, 29).

of knowledge to grace and of knowledge to prayer. This is clear: if what has been said of the relativity of all *rationes* is in fact true, then knowledge must be sought in prayer in the manner of *Prosl. 1*—however confident we may be in the *ratio* of the object of faith, however assured of our integrity in using our power of reason correctly. And as in that case knowledge is sought in prayer, so prayer can be made only if what has been said about the relativity of all *rationes* is in fact true.

2. Therefore, because it is truth that disposes of all *rationes* and not *vice versa*, the revelation must ensue first and foremost in the form of authority, in the form of the outward text: above all the *ratio veritatis* can be nothing more than something dictated. Then the human capacity for reason itself becomes a *vera ratio* when it is used in conformity with this something dictated. Just at this point the conception is somewhat remote, as if the 'faith under authority' (faith is always 'faith under authority') were an 'irrational' attitude. Yet in obeying the authority he is assuredly asserting the hidden *ratio* of the object of faith in order thereby to face and take up a problem presented to the human *ratio*.

3. One form of the revelation is obviously also the occurrence of *intelligere*, of the *vera ratione quaerere veram rationem*, the *intus legere*, to which even the inner text discloses itself, inasmuch as the conformity of *ratio* to truth depends neither upon the object nor the subject but on that same revealing power of God which illumines faith and which faith encounters as authority. The antithesis between *auctoritas* and *ratio* does not coincide with the antithesis between God and man but represents the distinction between two stages of the one divine road along which man first attains faith and then on the basis of faith (but now *sola ratione*) attains knowledge.

Our further examination of the concept of *ratio* must take into consideration its relation to the concept of *necessitas* which in Anselm we find invariably connected with it. In speaking of the objective *ratio*, the *ratio* proper to the object of faith, Anselm has connected *ratio* and *necessitas* by *et*[1] and in the same chapter by *vel* and by *et*.[2] Yet even at points where we would expect *ratio* as a description of the object that is sought or found, he has simply used *necessitas*.[3] And even when speaking of the subjective *ratio* which has to be achieved or is achieved dialectically he has equated *ratio* and *necessitas*[4] and interpreted *ratio* by *necessitas*[5] and *necessitas* by *ratio*.[6] I find it both possible and necessary to make the following comment on these remarkable facts:

Necessitas undoubtedly means the attribute of being unable not to be, or of being unable to be different. Among the many possible meanings of *ratio* in an author who continually employs the concept subjectively and objectively and in addition in this context uses it for *necessitas*, the one that is most highly recommended as a general guide is conformity to law.

There follow therefore in respect of the object of faith and in respect of knowledge of it the following definitions of *necessitas* and *ratio*:

(1) The *necessitas* that is peculiar to the object of faith is the impossibility of the object of faith not existing or of being otherwise than it is. The *necessitas* is its basis inasmuch as it does not permit it to change or to cease to exist.

(2) The *necessitas* that is peculiar to knowledge of the object of faith is the impossibility for thought to conceive the object of faith as not existing or as existing differently. The *necessitas* establishes this knowledge in so far as it is the negation achieved

---

1 *Qualiter mors illa rationabilis et necessaria monstrari possit* (C.D.h. I 10: II 66, 19f).

2 *Ibid. I 1:* II 48, 2 and 22.

3 *Est igitur ex necessitate aliqua natura . . .* (Monol. 4: I 17, 8f). *Si ergo cogitari potest esse (sc. Deus), ex necessitate est* (C. Gaun. 1: I 131, 5). *Monstratur . . . ex necessitate omnia quae de Christo credimus, fieri oportere* (C.D.h. Preface: II 43, 2f). *Probes Deum fieri hominem ex necessitate (ibid. II 22:* II 133, 6), etc. This naturally includes the frequent *necesse est* used to conclude proofs and sections of proofs.

4 *Veritatis solidatis rationabilis, id est necessitas* (C.D.h. I 4 : II 52, 3f).

5 *Ratio necessaria (ibid. I 25:* II 96, 2; *et al.,* also in the plural). *Rationem . . . comitatur necessitas (ibid. I 10 :* II 67, 5f).

6 *Rationis necessitas (Monol. Prologue: I 7,* 10); *rationabilis necessitas (C.D.h. I 25:* II 96, 10; *ibid. II 15 :* II 115, 24; *De proc. Spir. 11:* II 209, 16).

by thought of the non-existence or different existence excluded by the *necessitas* of the object of faith.

(3) The *ratio* that is peculiar to the object of faith is the fact that its existence conforms to law and that it exists in this particular way. The *ratio* is the rationality of the object in so far as it makes it intelligible to a being who can understand an existence and a particular existence that conform to law.

(4) The *ratio* peculiar to the knowledge of the object of faith is the conception of the conformity to law of the existence and particular existence of the object of faith taken up into the conception of the object of faith itself. The *ratio* is the understanding of this knowledge in so far as it characterizes it as the understanding of the object of faith by a being capable of comprehending an existence and a particular existence that conform to law.

From the relation of Definitions 1 and 2 to one another it follows:

(5) The establishing of knowledge of the object of faith consists in recognition of the basis that is peculiar to the object of faith itself. Ontic necessity precedes noetic.

From the relation of Definitions 3 and 4 to one another it follows:

(6) The element of reason in the knowledge of the object of faith consists in recognition of the rationality that is peculiar to the object of faith itself. Ontic rationality precedes noetic.

Anselm's frequent habit of interchanging *necessitas* and *ratio* justifies the following conclusions:

(7) The basis peculiar to the object of faith is consistent with its own particular rationality; ontic necessity is consistent with ontic rationality.

(8) The distinctive way in which knowledge of the object of faith is established is consistent with its own particular rationality; noetic necessity is consistent with noetic rationality.

From 5 and 7 it follows:

(9) Ontic necessity precedes even noetic rationality: the rationality of the object of faith also consists in the recognition of its own basis.

From 6 and 8 it follows:

(10) Ontic rationality precedes noetic necessity; the establishing of knowledge of the object of faith consists also in the recognition of the rationality belonging to the object of faith.

However, from what was said earlier about the relation of ontic and noetic *ratio* to *veritas* it follows:

(11) As ontic rationality is itself not an ultimate but is only true rationality measured alongside the *summa veritas*, the same is true of the ontic necessity that is consistent with it.[1] It is in the Truth and by the Truth, in God and by God that the basis is a basis and that rationality possesses rationality.

On the mutual relationship between necessity and rationality this has to be said:

(12) Inasmuch as the concept of necessity, though as substantiation it has noetic content too, possesses original affinity with the ontic and inasmuch as the concept of rationality, though as reasonableness it has ontic content too, possesses original affinity with the noetic—to that extent necessity must precede rationality. We see the same result if we take the problem back to the concept of truth. In so far as Anselm[2] clearly interprets truth in terms of *rectitudo* but on the other hand interprets righteousness[3] in terms of itself, he subordinates the knowledge of God to the will of God.

---

[1] *Deus nihil facit necessitate quia nullo modo cogitur aut prohibetur facere aliquid.* A *necessitas* that exists for God could only be the *immutabilitas honestatis eius, quam a se ipso et non ab alio habet et idcirco improprie dicitur necessitas* (*C.D.h. II 5:* II 100, 20ff). *Ille maxime laudandus est de bonis, quae habet et servat non ulla necessitate sed . . . propria et aeterna immutabilitate* (*ibid. II 10:* II 108, 7f; cf. *ibid. II 16-17*). *Omnis necessitas . . . eius* (*sc. Dei*) *subiacet voluntati. Quippe quod vult, necesse est esse* (*Medit. 3:* III 86, 60f; . . *Medit. 11* in *MPL* 158, 764). Ontic necessity is ascribed for example in *Cur Deus homo* to the incarnation and to the atoning death of Christ. It should never have been overlooked that ontic necessity in Anselm can as little be a final word as any other word that is not the inexpressible Word of the One and Only God, glorious in himself. *Si vis omnium quae fecit et quae passus est veram scire necessitatem, scito omnia ex necessitate fuisse, quia ipse voluit. Voluntatem vero eius nulla praecessit necessitas* (*C.D.h. II 17:* II 125, 28ff).

[2] *De verit. 11f:* I 191ff.   [3] Cf. also *De conc. virg. 3:* II 142f; *De lib. arb. 3:* I 210ff.

We summarize:

(13) It also follows from a consideration of the parallel conception to *ratio*, the conception of *necessitas*, that the 'rational' knowledge of the object of faith is derived from the object of faith and not *vice versa*. That means to say that the object of faith and its knowledge are ultimately derived from Truth, that is, from God and from his will.

(14) The concept *necessitas*, however, explains what is meant by 'rational' knowledge. When Anselm tries *ratione*, that is with his reason (by means of the capacity of comprehending existence and a particular existence as conforming to law), to apprehend noetically the *rationem fidei*, that is the rationality of the object of faith (its power of being understood by a being capable of comprehending existence and a particular existence that conforms to law), what he is trying to do is this: to conceive *necessitatem*, that is the basis of the object of faith (the impossibility of its not existing or of its existing differently), *necessitate*; to conceive it 'with reason' (conceiving the impossibility of its not existing or of its existing differently). That the object of faith has such a basis that it is impossible for it not to exist or to exist differently is for him given in the revelation and is certain in faith. His starting point is therefore not to seek 'what can be' but to seek 'what is' and in fact to seek 'what cannot fail to be'. It is precisely as 'what cannot fail to be' that he tries to conceive 'what is'. Corresponding to the basis in faith there has to be a reason in knowledge; to the ontic a corresponding noetic necessity. The way to the latter he finds in the confidence based on faith and faith alone that there might be a valid use of the human capacity to form concepts and judgments and that therefore there could be a valid noetic rationality (an understanding of existence and particular existence conforming to law). This could correspond to ontic rationality (to the rationality of the object of faith) and in virtue of this combination of ontic rationality and ontic necessity (rationality and basis of the object of faith) could

even bring to light the noetic necessity that is sought (the reason). With the proviso that truth itself is sovereign, Anselm has been successful in his search for the *intelligere* of this noetic rationality which is in fact aimed at noetic necessity by the roundabout argument for the rationality and necessity of the object.

How Anselm's struggle for this noetic rationality and therefore for the perception of the existence and particular existence of the object of faith was worked out *in concreto* has now to be shown.

From the whole tenor of his treatment of the problem as we have seen it up till now, we would expect his concern to be to meditate from time to time upon a particular article of the Christian *Credo*, that is to investigate the meaning of what it contains that he may place it in its relation to all the other articles or to the one next to it, comparing and connecting it with them and allowing them to illumine it. All this he does with the intention of himself conceiving by reflection the hidden law of the object of faith about which this article speaks, that thereby he may show it forth and so be able to know the thing believed: the noetic *ratio* leads to the discovery of the ontic *ratio* in so far as it follows after it;[1] in which case the remaining articles of the *Credo* point the way along which the noetic precedes the ontic *ratio*, along which the ontic *ratio* has to follow to discover it.[2]

Or should Anselm have thought of it all quite differently— at least parts of it occasionally? Should he really have sought the law of the existence and particular existence of the object of faith in the human capacity to form concepts and judgments (as identical with its laws) and therefore assumed as possible and necessary an independent knowledge alongside that of faith, able to draw from its own sources? Should he therefore

[1] We may think of the literal meaning of the verb '*investigare*' which Anselm liked to use to describe his researches (e.g. *Monol.* 1: I 13, 14)—'to follow a trail' (e.g. used of a dog on the scent).

[2] That therefore means: *ratione ducente et illo prosequente* (*Monol.* 1: I 13, 15f).

have begun *quaerens intellectum* with nothing, that is with the rules of an autonomous human reason and with the data of general human experience, and therefore of his own accord as *inveniens intellectum*, that is by means of certain universal 'necessities of thought' (comparable to Pharaoh's magicians), not so much have found but rather have created a kind of shadow *Credo*?.

To save repetition we shall have to say: nothing less than everything that we have so far established from Anselm's actual text with regard to the presuppositions, conditions and the nature of Anselm's *intelligere* testifies against the possibility of accepting such a view even in part.[1] And in fact it also lays itself open to direct refutation. We may recall what Anselm himself has said about his procedure. He declares, for example, his intention to lead the Greeks *rationabiliter* to insight into the '*filioque*' and continues that he will do this in such a way as to apply what they believe to the proof of what they do not believe.[2] So too in one of his later works he drew the limits of his task in this way: it would be valid for demonstrating the consistency of the doctrine of predestination with the doctrine of free-will to assume the validity of both.[3] The decisive proof against the alleged 'rationalism' of Anselm is most certainly, as we have already mentioned once before, what he has in actual fact said in his writings. As far as I am aware no one has ever yet tried to assert that the 'arguments' brought forward in his treatment of, say, the Incarnation of the Word, or of the relation of 'Nature' and 'Persons' in God, or of the coming of the Holy Spirit from the Father and from the Son, of the Virgin

---

[1] It reduces the theology of Anselm (shocking example: H. Reuter, *Geschichte der religiösen Aufklärung im Mittelalter*, vol. I, 1875, pp. 297f) to a labyrinth of arbitrariness or inconsequence and has no basis in his texts viewed as a whole, however easy it may be to misunderstand him in this direction from isolated passages read out of the context of this whole.

[2] *Graecorum fide atque iis quae credunt indubitanter et confitentur, pro certissimis argumentis ad probandum quod non credunt utar* (*De proc. Spir.* Prologue: II 177, 15ff).

[3] *Ponamus igitur simul esse et praescientiam . . . et libertatem . . . et videamus utrum impossibile sit, haec duo simul esse* (*De concordia* Qu. I 1: II 246, 2ff).

Birth and inherited sin, or of the fall of Lucifer—that these 'arguments' are rational grounds in the sense of inferences from general truths. But throughout all Anselm's investigation the origin of the *rationes necessariae* is to be found somewhere other than where it ought to be found in a philosopher who deduces the *Credo a priori*—namely, on the same level as that on which the question to be answered is raised, within the *Credo* itself. Within it, now this Article and now that Article figures as the unknown *X* which is solved in the investigation by means of the Articles of faith *a, b, c, d* . . . which are assumed to be known (without assuming knowledge of *X* and to that extent *sola ratione*). The inquiring theologian, with his capacity for forming concepts and making judgments, is never assigned the function of determining the fixed point or fixed points from which the argument is to proceed. His function is rather as follows: on the one hand, a selection from among the points fixed previously (elsewhere, or in another way); and on the other hand— and this is his proper task—the formulation, according to the rules of logic based upon the law of contradiction (and within the limits it permits), of the definitions, conclusions, differentiations and correlations necessary for the resolution of that *X*. And so—not mastering the object but being mastered by it—he achieves true noetic *ratio*, a real comprehension of the ontic *ratio* of the object of faith; he attains to the *intellectus fidei*. Even in the *Cur Deus homo*—the writing which at this point we regard as the one most open to dispute—it is exactly the same. The vital presuppositions which underlie the demonstration of the rationality, or rather, the necessity, of the Incarnation and of the atoning Death of Christ are: continuity between a divine purpose and the human race,[1] the obligation essential to the nature of man to obey God,[2] sin as man's eternal guilt before God,[3] the inviolability of God's negation of sin,[4] man's inability to save himself[5] and last but not least—the aseity and

---

[1] *C.D.h. I 4, 16–19, 23; II 1.*   [2] *Ibid. I 20.*   [3] *Ibid. I 11, 21; II 11, 14.*
[4] *Ibid. I 8, 12–15, 24; II 20.*   [5] *Ibid. I 24.*

'honour' of God expressed in the Creation Dogma, which in all contexts permits, one might say 'requires', Anselm to apply the criterion of what is or is not 'fitting' for God.[1] These are the *a, b, c, d* . . . from which points the *X*, which on this occasion is a Christological *X*,[2] will be shown to be 'rational' or 'necessary'.[3] This position comes out much more clearly in the *Monologion*[4] and in the second part of the *Proslogion*, not to mention just yet *Prosl. 2-4*. In both these places Anselm deals with—admittedly a particularly awkward theme—the Being of God. The question may be seriously asked whether at least in these writings[5] he has not indulged in *a priori* theology. Even here I would say not, though I would not dispute the existence of a certain lack of clarity in method. The road taken by Anselm's later writings (and it is in *Cur Deus homo* that this is most clearly seen), leads in the opposite direction. Anselm could not have remained ignorant of so serious a break in his development[6] or failed to give some kind of indication of it. But in none of his letters and writings have we a trace of evidence for

---

[1] *In Deo quamlibet parvum inconveniens sequitur impossibilitas* (*ibid. I 10:* II 67 4f).

[2] Described by that *remoto Christo* which we have already mentioned (cf. p. 43). It means: precisely because on this occasion the point at issue is the proof of the rationality and necessity of the Person and Work of Christ, the space which it receives in Scripture, in the *Credo* and in Christian experience on this occasion is to be filled up; that is, the arguments based thereon are this time to be left out of account.

[3] Hence this concentration of the inquiry on this problem—*Non enim proposuimus tractare nisi de sola incarnatione* (cf. also *ibid. I 10:* II 67, 9f)—does not stop Anselm, following Boso's encouragement *hilarem datorem diligit Deus* (*ibid. I 16:* II 74, 15ff) also illustrating in the same way at least in passing the rationality or necessity of certain neighbouring points in the *Credo* (here belongs *inter alia* the long excursus on the eschatological Kingdom of Spirits, *I 16-19*, which at the time Anselm had omitted from the recapitulation of *Cur Deus homo* given in *Medit. 3—11* in *MPL*) —so that at the end Boso—perhaps not without humour slightly tinged by schoolboy optimism—can be of the opinion: *per unius quaestionis quam proposuimus solutionem, quidquid in novo veterique testamento continetur, probatum intelligo* (*ibid. II 22:* II 133, 4f).

[4] I could not agree with the verdict of F. R. Hasse (*Anselm of Canterbury*, vol 2, 1852, p. 114): 'This his first work is easily the simplest to understand; none other is better thought out, more uniformly constructed or more carefully expounded.' On the contrary, I think that in the *Monologion* Anselm had not yet quite found his feet.

[5] They fit into the early period of his activity as Prior at Bec (1063-78).

[6] We may think of his tactical situation over against the actual rationalists of his time.

that conclusion. My view is then that even in the *Monologion* we are confronted by a very pronounced rejection of speculation that does not respect the incomprehensibility of the reality of the object of faith,[1] by a recognition of the indirectness of all knowledge of God,[2] and also, though more clearly than in the *Proslogion*, by the reference to the Pattern of faith which is the basis of everything.[3] When at the beginning Anselm declared himself capable of bringing to an understanding of the Nature of God even a person to whom the *Credo* has until now been foreign either because he was not acquainted with it or because he did not believe it,[4] that cannot mean (compare *cap. 64*) that by such instruction he could create either for that man or for himself a substitute for the knowledge of faith. In laying hold of the Word Anselm has left behind him the unbridgeable gulf between an understanding of the divine Being that can be attained if need be without faith and the affirmation of this Being carried out in spite of, and with, the basic inconceivability of its *quomodo*. It is from this point that his teaching begins and it is there alone that instruction can take place that would make possible advances to the solution of other questions as well. It is in this way that the development of *Monol. 1-6*, which is frequently though erroneously (on account of the memory of Thomas Aquinas) described as the 'Cosmological Proof of the Existence of God', will be understood. In the controversy with Gaunilo Anselm expressly described the procedure that is used here—of ascending from the conception of the relative Good, Great and Existent Being which confronts us in the world to that of a final and real, indeed a single Good, Great and Existent Being—as a *conicere* such that the question *sive sit in re aliquid huius modi* might remain an open question.[5] That, however, means—by presupposing the question, to be clarified elsewhere, about the Existence of God, the Nature of God is to be elucidated here in the *Monologion* (actually in a way that the religiously ignorant can

---

[1] *Monol. 64.*   [2] *Ibid. 65.*   [3] *Ibid. 76f.*   [4] *Ibid. 1.*   [5] *C. Gaun. 8:* I 137, 23f.

understand). But the Existence of God, which then in *Prosl 2-4* itself becomes the problem, is not all in the *Monologion* that is taken as 'believed', as to be examined elsewhere. Behind *Monol. 1-6* there stands (thus also explaining *cap. 7-8*) the dogma of the creation out of nothing; behind the doctrine of the attributes of God[1] (despite all the Neo-Platonic technique in the exposition) there stands the Christian avowal of the Unity and Omnipotence of God; behind the doctrine of the Divine Word[2] there is naturally the Christology of the Roman Catholic Church, which we cannot discuss here. And if Anselm, in explaining the Doctrine of the Trinity,[3] adduces the well-known Augustinian *vestigium trinitatis* (*memoria, intelligentia, amor*) as the image of God in man and therefore as the nearest and best basis of knowledge,[4] that also meant for him at least, as we also can take it to mean, a 'biblical-ecclesiastical-dogmatic' presupposition and not an instance of 'natural' theology, of a second theology alongside the one Revealed Theology. In the second part of the *Proslogion* (apart from what it has in common with the *Monologion*) Anselm's 'rationalism' would have to be sought in the closer systematic which he attained by the application of the *unum argumentum* (*id quo maius cogitari nequit*) that he had meanwhile discovered. But this very *argumentum* is again inexplicable if combined with Creation[5] and God's Unity and Aseity.[6] The deliberations on the relation of Mercy and Impassivity[7] and of Mercy and Righteousness in God[8] assumed the questions of *Cur Deus homo* to be answered, and the expositions on God's Hiddenness and Incomprehensibility[9] remind us again of the reality of the Revelation which cannot be analysed by any causal or teleological construction but which is rational and necessary in itself. Finally, we may recall the *credo ut intelligam*, so unambiguous (unlike Augustine's), at the beginning of this very work and also the remarkable

---

[1] *Monol 15-24.*   [2] *Ibid. 9-14, 29-37.*   [3] *Ibid. 29-65.*
[4] *Ibid. 47-48, 66-68.*   [5] *Prosl. 3.*   [6] *Ibid. 5.*
[7] *Ibid. 8.*   [8] *Ibid. 9-11.*   [9] *Ibid. 14-17.*

form of adoration with which Anselm embellished his argument just at this point. Strange indeed the contradiction if, against such a background, what he had intended to say about God were something his thinking had created rather than something received. However interesting for a study of his procedural technique[1] the reference to his inevitable philosophical ancestry (Augustine, Plotinus, Plato) may be, so far as the contents of his 'proofs' are concerned, there is absolutely no valid reason against, and a great many reasons for, understanding him theologically as a descendant of this line. The Proof of the Existence of God in *Prosl. 2-4*, on which we have not yet embarked here, would be completely anomalous if it were to be understood in any other way.

5. THE AIM OF THEOLOGY (THE PROOF)

Right at the outset of our inquiry, in anticipation, we established that Anselm speaks of 'proofs' when he has in mind a particular result, namely, the polemical-apologetical result of his theological work. In so far as there is knowledge it issues in proof and proof is, as it were, the highest reach of knowledge. And Anselm wants to prove.[2] Of course he wants to do more than prove. He is also interested, as we saw, in the *pulchritudo* of the completed knowledge. But he still wants to prove. His thinking is done in relation to One whom he is to address and who stands over against the merely human. In the *Monologion* we hear the voice of a *persona secum sola cogitatione disputantis et investigantis.*[3] But as we saw, the adoption of the dialogue form

[1] In this connection cf. Alexandre Koyré, *L'idée de Dieu dans la philosophie de St. Anselme*, Paris 1923.

[2] For example, according to a later statement of his own in the *Monologion* and *Proslogion*—to prove: *quod fide tenemus de divina natura et eius personis* (*Ep. de incarn. 6:* II 20, 18) or, the Western *Filioque* (*De proc. Spir. 1:* II 177, 16) or, the necessity of the incarnation of Christ (*C.D.h. II 22:* II 133, 6).

[3] *Monol. Prologue:* I 8, 18f—as far as I can see, according to *Monol. 1* even this solitary Christian thinker occupies himself very vigorously with the possibilities of what is non-Christian.

did not mean that he was renouncing such thinking in solitude. For that reason it is therefore significant. He knows, and he knows that his readers know, that the Articles of the Christian *Credo* are misunderstood, doubted and disputed by heathens, Jews and heretics and that even where that is not so, within the Church itself, its *ratio* is sought not without some anxiety.[1] In coming-to-grips with this situation Anselm's *intelligere* is realized, and to that extent *probare* is achieved.

If we want to understand what 'proofs' means here the first thing that has to be observed is that the *ratio veritatis* inherent in the Articles of the Christian *Credo* is itself at no point the subject of discussion but on the contrary it forms the self-evident basis of discussion. The dialogue form and the desire for proof in no sense indicate that Anselm has accepted a position where faith and unbelief, the voice of the Church and every other voice, have equal rights. The reason which Anselm occasionally gives for choosing this particular dialogue form certainly does not suggest that the Archbishop of Canterbury ever had the slightest intention of vacating his *cathedra* even temporarily for the purposes of this discussion.[2] And secondly, Boso who feigns to oppose and ask questions takes up his position—the same is in effect true of the *discipulus* in the other dialogues—expressly on the basis of Anselm's *credo ut intelligam*,[3] explains his wonted representation of the 'unbelieving' as a 'mask'[4] and at the same time, as already noticed, represents the interest of ecclesiastical authority as against theology. Obviously this is no free school of free convictions. The relation between Anselm

[1] *C.D.h. Preface:* II 42, 9ff; *ibid. I 1:* II 47, 11–48, 2; *ibid. II 22:* II 133, 8. *Ep. de incarn. 1:* II 6, 2f.

[2] *Quoniam ea, quae per interrogationem et responsionem investigantur, multis et maxime tardioribus ingeniis magis patent et ideo plus placent (C.D.h. I 1:* II 48, 11ff).

[3] *C.D.h. I 1:* II 48, 16ff. Anselm starts off on the assumption that he is asked *ex caritate et religioso studio (ibid. I 2:* II 50, 3f).

[4] *Patere igitur, ut verbis utar infidelium. Aequum enim est, ut cum nostrae fidei rationem studemus inquirere, ponam eorum obiectiones (ibid. I 3:* II 50, 16f). *Accipis in hac quaestione personam eorum qui credere nihil volunt . . . (ibid. I 10:* II 67, 1f).

and Gaunilo, the monk of Marmoutiers and critic of section *2-4* of the *Proslogion*, is exactly the same. Gaunilo is far from being an atheist.[1] Not only does he expressly[2] declare his agreement with all the other parts of the *Proslogion* but he also describes the first part of the work which he challenges as *recte quidem sensa*, even if *minus firmiter argumentata*, so that with that reservation he considers that he can and ought to assent to the whole.[3] Thus it is not the existence of God that he discusses but only the proof that Anselm gives for it. He too, writes, as is expressly confirmed by Anselm, not as *insipiens*, but as *catholicus* even if as *catholicus pro insipiente*.[4] Thus no part of the entire edifice of the Church is for a single moment in jeopardy. Concerning the objective rationality of faith Anselm neither regards himself as having been asked nor bound to give any account. No doubt it was only with the greatest surprise that he faced the imputation that in this matter the theologian too must have his 'anxiety': apart from the appropriately ecclesiastical assumption of this objective rationality, all the trouble over *intelligere* as well as all the questions and answers of theological polemic and apologetic had neither meaning nor object. On the assumption that it is true to say: God exists, God is the highest Being, is a Being in Three Persons; became man, etc.—Anselm discusses the question of how far it is true and in asking and allowing himself to be asked about this 'how far' in respect of particular articles of faith, in his answers he takes as his starting-point the

[1] Note his sentence meant in all seriousness: *Summum illud quod est, scilicet Deus, et esse et non esse non posse indubitanter intelligo (Pro insip. 7:* I 129, 15f).

[2] Indeed, with an extravagance that is almost suspicious: *Cetera libelli illius tam veraciter et tam praeclare sunt magnificeque disserta, tanta denique referta utilitate et pii ac sancti affectus intimo quodam odore fragrantia* . . . (*Pro. insip. 8:* I 129, 20ff). Did Gaunilo already admire to some extent Anselm's 'piety' so as to be able to dispense with his theology with more confidence?

[3] *Omnia cum ingenti veneratione et laude suscipienda (Pro insip. 8:* I 129, 24f).

[4] *C. Gaun. Prologue:* I 130, 4f—in view of this little Prologue and in view of the remaining content of Anselm's answer it is absolutely impossible, following P. Daniels (P. Augustinus Daniels, O.S.B., *Quellenbeiträge und Untersuchungen zur Geschichte der Gottesbeweise im 13. Jahrhundert*, Münster 1909), to give to this work the title 'Contra insipientem' (even if there were any manuscript evidence available—a conclusion not to be gathered from Daniel's exposition on p. 3). This title cannot be Anselm's.

assumption that all the other articles are true. Thus his conception of *intelligere* must obviously, if he is not going to contradict himself completely, be his conception of *probare* as well. The anxiety regarding the 'how far' is enough; for the difficulties brought up by the others and still more those of which he is sufficiently aware himself are really serious. This anxiety is appropriate and significant. It is to be accepted by any conscientious inquiry that does not ignore even the most obviously superficial and indeed stupid opposition, that in its progress leaves behind nothing that is unexplained[1] and that is not content[2] merely to uncover formal analogies (*convenientiae*). There is added anxiety with regard to the uncertainty and the limited nature of all human knowledge, regarding the genuineness of the act of faith that forms the basis of knowledge and finally regarding the gracious presence of God which first makes it real and which has ever and anew to be sought. Uncertainty as to whether in Holy Scripture or in the *Credo* God has done his work well; uncertainty because of the existence of the unbelieving, that is of other religions or of heresy; serious consideration of the possibility of rejecting revelation— none of these in any sense belong to the presuppositions of Anselm's Proof.

There is therefore a special significance in the one who stands over against the heathen, Jew or heretic to whom the Proof is addressed. There is no question but that this other person who rejects the Christian revelation and therefore Anselm's presupposition, is really before Anselm's mind as he writes and that he is speaking in opposition to him, addressing him, wishing to say something to him or at least wishing to reduce him to silence. Certainly not one of Anselm's writings appeals to us as being addressed directly to those outside that is as 'apologetic'

---

[1] *Nullam vel simplicem paeneque fatuam objectionem disputanti mihi occurentem negligendo volo praeterire. Quatenus et ego nihil ambiguum in praecedentibus relinquens certior valeam ad sequentia procedere et si cui forte quod speculor persuadere voluero, omni vel modico remoto obstaculo quilibet tardus intellectus ad audita facile possit accedere* (Monol. 6: 1 19, 16ff; cf. ibid. Prologue: 1 7, 11f).

[2] C.D.h. I 3-4.

in the modern sense. The readers whom he visualizes and for whom he caters are the Christian theologians, or more exactly, the Benedictine theologians of his day.[1] Anselm's theology is therefore no esoteric wisdom; it develops—we will have to say, 'usually'—as the rendering of an account against *omni poscenti se rationem de ea quae in nobis est spe*.[2] It is the denial that more or less assumes the role of partner in the discussion.[3] But that is not to say that he felt compelled to take up his position on his opponent's ground. He could not do that and he did not do it. As soon as he formulated his polemical-apologetic programme thus—'it is right *insipienter quaerenti sapienter respondere*'[4] or again '*rationabiliter ostendendum est, quam irrationabiliter nos contemnant*'[5]—the opposites *sapientia* and *insipientia*, *rationabilitas* and *irrationabilitas* make it quite clear that the parties in the discussion are operating on two very different planes. And if in these passages we are not to understand such a complex concept as *ratio* in a non-dialectic, subjective sense, in accordance with certain necessary associations that emanate from the eighteenth century, but rather in the same vigorous sense in which, according to our argument, it is used elsewhere in Anselm, then surely it is impossible that all of a sudden at this point Anselm should have conceded to the non-believer (and to himself as well) a noetic rationability without its being conditioned by an ontic one, that is without its being ulti-. mately conditioned by the *summa veritas* and therefore without revelation, grace and faith—in order to embark arm in arm with the unbeliever on an arbitrary reconstruction, 'from pure reason', of the Christian knowledge and so to surrender to him the required proof for the *ratio fidei*. Just as Anselm holds that

---

[1] Compare in this respect Daniels, pp. 112f.   [2] *C.D.h. I 1*: II 47, 10f.

[3] *Fides nostra contra impios ratione defendenda est* (*Ep. 136:* III 280, 34f). *Ille insipiens, contra quem sum locutus in meo opusculo* ... (*C. Gaun. Prologue:* I 130, 3f).

[4] *De casu diab. 27:* I 275, 5.

[5] *Ep. 136:* III 281, 37f; or: the unbeliever is to be trained *ad ea, quae irrationabiliter ignorat, rationabiliter proficere* (*Monol. 1:* I 13, 16) or: *ratione qua se* (sc. *infidelis*) *defendere nititur, eius error demonstrandus est* (*Ep. de incarn. 2:* II 11, 7f).

there is no self-redemption of any sort[1] so he also holds that there is none from *irrationabilitas* to *rationabilitas*, and from *insipientia* to *sapientia*. But on the contrary, when it happens that the noetic *ratio* rises out of *irrationabilitas* and therefore becomes *vera ratio* then this is the work of the self-illuminating *ratio veritatis* which illumines the noetic *ratio* from above, that is, it is the work of the *ratio fidei* itself. In this all that we can do from the human side is to try to explore this *ratio* to the best of our knowledge and conscience with the aid of the documents of revelation, and so to bring it before our opponent as something that has been investigated in order that it might speak for itself and might speak directly to him. Anselm also regards the 'unbelievers' as suffering from the fact that they forego this human assistance. Not being in a position to study the *ratio fidei* itself and no one else having done this work for them, they certainly hear the message of the Christian *Credo* but its meaning strikes them as being contrary to reason or *vice versa*.[2] They want to know about this *ratio* first before they believe it.[3] Clearly in this latter respect Anselm can have no desire to help them. As theology cannot anticipate the transformation of *insipiens* into *fidelis* so now with a believer's knowledge neither can it expect to dissolve the *rectus ordo* of the relation between faith and knowledge by virtue of which faith is obedience to authority which must be prior to knowledge.[4] If that transformation did not take place and therefore this obedience did not occur all that would remain between Anselm and his opponent would be a gulf (from each side of which two totally different things are being said in the same language),

---

[1] *Nec enim convertere me possum ad te tot et tantis vulneribus et aegritudinibus et morte ipsa depressus et impotens effectus. Sed tu, misericors Pater, converte me, et convertar ad te* (*Medit. 8: MPL* 158, 747f).

[2] *Infideles Christianam fidem quia rationi putant illam repugnare respuentes* . . . (*C.D.h.* Preface: II 42, 10f). *Nequaquam enim acquiescunt multi Deum aliquid velle, si ratio repugnare videtur* (*ibid. I 8:* II 59, 12f).

[3] *Qui nullatenus ad fidem eandem sine ratione volunt accedere* (*ibid. I 3:* II 50, 17f). *Qui credere nihil volunt, nisi praemonstrata ratione* (*ibid. I 10:* II 67, 1f).

[4] *C.D.h. I 1:* II 48, 16.

over which therefore neither help nor agreement is possible.[1] The inexplicable possibility exists that the partner in discussion is and remains an *insipiens*, in which case all discussion with him is pointless and meaningless. Were Anselm to reckon *in concreto* with the given-ness of this possibility he could obviously do nothing but abandon the attempt, only just begun, to give human assistance to his partner. If, in the last analysis, this partner is completely devoid of faith, then any attempt to help him in regard to knowledge of faith, of which of course he must also be devoid, cannot but be in vain. And so *insipienter quaerere* and *sapienter respondere* are marching along side by side but really having nothing in common and once that is recognized they might as well save themselves all the trouble and excitement.

But now we come to the exceedingly remarkable fact that Anselm did not reckon with the given-ness of that possibility, or at least made no use of such a notion.[2] It has often been noted that Anselm's writings, whose purposes have frequently been compared to those of the Crusades,[3] are on the other hand distinguished by an extraordinary mildness when it comes to polemics.[4] This can and must be understood partly

[1] The incomprehensibility of predestination corresponds to the incomprehensibility of the factuality of the revelation: Anselm sees *mixtim et iustorum et iniustorum infantes ad baptismi gratiam eligi et ab illa reprobari* (*De conc. virg. 24:* II 167, 17f) and in face of this mystery can offer neither explanation nor advice: *Illud certe nulla ratione comprehendi potest, cur de similibus malis hos magis salves quam illos per summam bonitatem et illos magis damnes quam istos per summam iustitiam* (*Prosl. 11:* I 109, 22ff).

[2] In my opinion it is touched on twice (that this can happen is worth noting): in the *quia insipiens est! ergo contemnendum est, quod dicit* (*C.D.h. I 25:* II 95, 20f) and likewise at the climax of the proof (*Prosl. 3:* I 103, 11). But in both passages it is abandoned at once.

[3] For example, F. Overbeck, *Vorgeschichte und Jugend der Mittelalterlichen Scholastik* 1917, pp. 228f. 1094-98 Anselm writes *Cur Deus homo.* 1095—Urban II calls for the first Crusade. 1099—Jerusalem is taken.

[4] The few exceptions where it rises to an effect bordering on anger are from another point of view characteristic—*Ep. de incarn 1* (II 9, 20ff)—he speaks quite angrily against the nominalistic-philosophical background of certain of his contemporaries—*Ep. 136* (III 280, 26ff)—he just cannot understand the effect of the 'Christian' heresy in view of baptism even the authors of the heresy share, in which. *C.D.h. II 10* (II 108, 20ff)—Boso is sharply rebuked because in discussing the problem of freedom he had cast up the question of why God did not create man like himself—immune from temptation.

in terms of personal psychology. But this mildness plus the fact that, apparently without the slightest inhibition, Anselm did in fact embark on the attempt to provide proof in face of unbelievers and false believers and despite the *Credo ut intelligam* and his predestinarian background, nevertheless requires some practical explanation. We can start from Anselm's astonishing recognition (put into the mouth of Boso) that what the believer and the unbeliever are meaning and seeking in their questions is exactly the same: *Quamvis enim illi ideo rationem quaerant, quia non credunt, nos vero, quia credimus: unum idemque tamen est, quod quaerimus.*[1] What does that mean? We know that Anselm's *quaerere rationem* means to show the noetic rationality of faith by explaining the mutual relations of the individual parts of the *Credo*. *Unum idemque est, quod quaerimus:* thus Anselm gives credit to the unbelievers to the extent that the *ratio* of faith which they lack and for which they ask is one and the same *ratio* as the one which he himself is seeking. It is not the revelation itself that offends them—if that happened then of course they would be *insipientes* and beyond help. Anselm does not burden them with this possibility. But leaving aside the question of revelation as such, they do take offence at some constituent part of the revelation because the context, the totality of the revelation is unknown to them and therefore this or that constituent part (not being illuminated by the whole) is beyond their comprehension. In face of the unbeliever's rock of offence thus understood, the Christian theologian does not feel himself powerless. Thus understood, it is in fact identical with the rock of offence by which he himself was driven and continues to be driven from *credere* to *intelligere*. Therefore all he has to do is to lead his opponent along his own path and thus be able to give him the answers to the questions that even he himself is asking. If such is Anselm's interpretation of the quest of the 'unbeliever' then we can understand how he comes to

[1] *C.D.h. I 3:* II 50, 18ff.

engage in a discussion with him without either accepting the unbeliever's criterion, such as universal human reason, or stipulating that the unbeliever in order to become competent to discuss must first be converted into a believer. Anselm assumes his own ground, the ground of strictly theological (we would nowadays say dogmatic) impartiality, to be likewise a ground on which the 'unbeliever' could quite well discuss and would want to discuss. Thus he summons him on to his own ground; or rather he addresses him as one who by his questions has already accepted this ground and therefore he is able (without renouncing the *credo ut intelligam* or his predestinarian background) to discuss with him as if he were a Boso or a Gaunilo.[1] Did Anselm really so interpret the unbeliever's quest? Again this must be settled one way or the other on an examination of the actual content of Anselm's writings. On that basis we must certainly say, 'Yes. Anselm has so interpreted this quest.' We will not find any passage in Anselm where he worked out the 'proof', that is the argument directed outwards with the unbeliever in view, as an action that is different from the searchings that take faith itself as starting-point or where another special 'apologetic' action would follow on the 'dogmatic' or where such action basing itself on or including the dogmatic action would come first anagogically or apagogically.[2] But even the working out of the *intelligere* of faith, even the inward proof, is also the outward proof. The unbeliever's quest is not simply taken up in any casual fashion and incorporated into the theological task but all the way through it is in fact treated as identical with the quest of the believer himself. Long before his 'unbelieving' partner in discussion ever appeared, Anselm most certainly intended to destroy the appearance of a *repugnare* between *ratio* and *fides*. It was and remains quite impossible for Anselm

---

[1] That is why he can even appoint his fellow-believer Boso as representative of the 'unbeliever'.

[2] It would have been quite impossible for Anselm to write a *Summa theologica* as well as a *Summa contra Gentiles*: a volume of Dogmatics as well as a Philosophy of Religion or the like.

to allow his faith to come to peaceable terms with lack of knowledge. What question of the unbeliever could be new to him and what answer could he give him save that which he gives to himself? Anselm's Proof works on the assumption that there is a solidarity between the theologian and the worldling which has not come about because the theologian has become one of the crowd, or one voice in a universal debating chamber, but because he is determined to address the worldling as one with whom he has at least this in common— theology. So he is able to promise him instruction on how he could convince himself, given a certain amount of intelligence, of the reasonableness of the Christian faith without having first accepted the truth of the revelation.[1] Fancy giving him such instruction as assumes Christian Dogma, although it is a matter of *quaerit, quia non credit*; the questioning is from one who is outside, indeed a 'spectator', and he not only doubts but denies and despises! But it is precisely this instruction which is provided for precisely this person!

Anselm's theology is simple. That is the plain secret of his 'proving'. Anselm is not in a position to treat Christian knowledge as an esoteric mystery, as a phenomenon that would have to shun the cold light of secular thinking. He credits his theology as such—without special adaptation for those outside —with being conclusive and convincing. He would have to distrust his theology and it would no longer be convincing even to himself and therefore it would be bad theology, if, for the benefit of those outside, he had to give precedence to special proofs over its own distinctive arguments. And Anselm is in no position to serve the world with something other than that with which he himself is served. Not only because he quite honestly has nothing else to offer or because he knows no other

---

[1] *Si quis . . . quae de Deo sive de eius creatura necessarie credimus, aut non audiendo aut non credendo ignorat: puto quia ea ipsa ex magna parte, si vel mediocris ingenii est, potest ipse sibi saltem sola ratione persuadere. Qnod cum multis modis facere possit, unum ponam . . .* then follows the 'Cosmological Proof of the Existence of God' (*Monol. 1:* I 13, 5ff), which has already been mentioned.

proof than the one that convinces him, but also because he knows himself to be responsible to the world and dares not offer it anything less than the best. And for that reason Anselm knows just one question, one language and one task of theology. He does not undertake his task without the intention of 'proving', which means wishing to make the Faith comprehensible to everyone, not only to himself, not only to the little flock but to everyone. But he can only prove on the basis of an investigation in strict theological neutrality, as if there were no rejection of the revelation and of dogma.

Thus there arises here a final enigma the statement (not the solution) of which may conveniently form the conclusion of this section. To say that with this procedure Anselm makes it easy for himself would obviously be far too foolish an objection to be worthy of lengthy refutation. Anyone who knows Anselm's proofs knows that he did not make it easy for himself. And the other possibility, the possibility of a discussion on the 'un-believer's ground, was for Anselm, be it 'easy' or 'difficult', excluded and forbidden—it was no possibility at all. No doubt, however, it can and must be asked, on the basis of his pre-supposition: is he not deceiving himself when he thinks that his 'proofs' could ever be understood by the unbelievers, by those who *quaerunt, quia non credunt,* and when he thinks that not only is theological discussion possible with them, but that it should succeed—the question of revelation and of faith always left open—in convincing them of the reasonableness of the *Credo*? What kind of unbelievers could he have had in mind who allow themselves to be transposed in this way *nolens volens* into the realm of theology? And was it not the case that his own *credo ut intelligam* was the best argument against the possibility of such uncommitted understanding, against the possibility of a *theologia irregenitorum,* a theological, non-Christian impartiality? And even at its best could the outcome of such instruction be anything but useless information about the inner consistency of Christian statements which would be completely incapable of preventing the person so informed from doubting, denying and despising the whole thing as much as ever and, with the whole thing, the details too? In what sense could this result, which it is highly improbable would be otherwise, be worth all the trouble expended on it? Is it not true that right from the start the whole attempt to prove was a false and reprehensible notion and would Anselm not have done better and remained truer to his own purposes had he given his theology the clear character of an esoteric science? To that we have the following to say: In the history of theology in all times and developments the *via regia* of divine simplicity and the way of the most incredible deception have always run parallel, separated only by the merest hair's breadth. It can never be at all evident in any statement of any theologian whether it stands on this or that side of the boundary. Therefore we are not to be surprised if we see the possibility of incredible deception apparently clear enough for us to spot even in the midst of the theology of Anselm. But we must also for that reason not blind ourselves to the possibility that what at first glance looks like incredible deception might in actual fact be divine simplicity which, not heeding the evil appearance, knows exactly what it wants and does not want and is surer of its goal than is realized by the all too hasty critic. That it means disaster for his entire undertaking is not the only view that we need take of Anselm's desire to prove: perhaps he was daring to assume that disbelief, the *quia non credimus*, the doubt, denial and derision of the unbeliever are not really to be taken so seriously as the unbeliever himself would take them. Perhaps, while appealing to him 'with proof', it was not in his lack of faith that he was trusting but in his faith. Perhaps he saw him standing at his side not only within the precincts of theology, but more important within the precincts of the Church. Because of some sort of quality encountered in the unbeliever? Perhaps because of some kind of power of his subjective *ratio* existing from creation and not obliterated by the Fall? Or, because of some vague, universal piousness possessed even by the natural man? These of course are possibilities totally foreign to Anselm and from a rational standpoint are to be discounted. It may be, however, that Anselm could quite well have risked that astonishing assumption because of the power of the objective *ratio* of the object of faith that enlightens and is enlightened from above by the *summa veritas* and which, according to Anselm, was able to teach and all along did teach truths that are beyond the power of one human being to teach another. Perhaps for Anselm theology had as much a part in proclaiming Christ as preaching, where the first and last presupposition of the preacher must be trust in the objective *ratio* that both enlightens and is enlightened, where consequently sins are not to be imputed, the sinner not to be held guilty for his sinfulness but in his sinfulness to be claimed for God, and where we must move on past the listener's tragic *non credo* to our task with a sense of humour, which in this instance is not only permissible but is actually demanded. Perhaps Anselm did not know any other way of speaking of the Christian *Credo* except by addressing the sinner as one who had not sinned, the non-Christian as a Christian, the unbeliever as believer, on the basis of the great 'as if' which is really not an 'as if' at all, but which at all times has been the final and decisive means whereby the believer could speak to the unbeliever. Perhaps, desiring to prove, he did not really remain standing on this side of the gulf between the believer and non-believer but crossed it, though on this occasion not in search of a truce as has been said of him and has often happened, but—here reminiscences of the days of the Crusaders could come to the fore—as conqueror whose weapon was the fact that he met the unbelievers as one of them and accepted them as his equal.[1]

---

[1] *Unde ego considerans quantum peccavi quantisque iniquitatibus infelix anima mea polluta sit, intelligo me non solum aequalem cum aliis peccatoribus sed plus quam ullum peccatorem et ultra omnes peccatores esse peccatorem* (*Medit. 6: MPL* 158, 739).

But we must not stretch this point any further. We can only say that if that is how Anselm thought then it was reasonable and so, dismissing the possibility that he was deceived, clearly his attitude to proving is exactly as we have seen.

II

THE PROOF OF THE EXISTENCE
OF GOD

A. The Presuppositions of the Proof

1. THE NAME OF GOD

In *Prosl. 2-4* Anselm wants to prove the existence of God. He proves it by assuming a Name of God the meaning of which implies that the statement 'God exists' is necessary (that means, that the statement 'God does not exist' is impossible). In *Prosl. 5-26* Anselm wants to prove the Nature of God (that means his Perfection and Unique Originality). He proves it on the presupposition of a Name of God, the meaning of which implies that the statements, 'God is perfect and originally wise, mighty, righteous, etc.,' are necessary (that is, all statements to the opposite effect are impossible). The lever in both cases, the *argumentum* in his analysis of both parts of the *Proslogion* is therefore the Name of God that is presupposed[1] concerning which the author tells us in the Prologue how he sought it and how, after he had abandoned the search, he suddenly found it.

At the beginning of *Prosl. 2*, where it appears for the first time, this Name is rendered by the words: *aliquid quo nihil cogitari possit*. The actual formulation is not fixed either in the *Proslogion* itself or in the essay against Gaunilo: instead of *aliquid* Anselm can also say *id*. It can even be further abbreviated by omitting the pronoun. *Possit* can be replaced by *potest* and occasionally

---

[1] *Tantam enim vim huius prolationis in se continet significatio* (that simply means the Name of God that is presupposed) *ut hoc ipsum quod dicitur, ex necessitate eo ipso quod intelligitur vel cogitatur et revera probetur existere et id ipsum esse quidquid de divina substantia oportet credere* (C. Gaun. *10:* 1 138, 30–139, 3).

73

by *valet*; *nihil* also by *non*; *nihil* (or *non*) . . . *possit* (or *potest*) also by *nequit* and also, quite frequently, by *maius* or *melius*. Only this last variant is important for an understanding of the formula. In the first place the literal meaning of the formula is clear. It can be quite easily translated into French: '*Un être tel qu'on n'en peut concevoir de plus grand*'[1] or even better, '*Quelque chose dont on ne peut rien concevoir de plus grand.*'[2] In German it can be paraphrased: '*Etwas über dem ein Grösseres nicht gedacht werden kann*'. (Something beyond which nothing greater can be conceived.) Here 'great' suggests, as is shown by the variant *melius* and by the whole application of the formula, quite generally the large mass of all the qualities of the object described and therefore as much its 'greatness' in relation to time and space as the 'greatness' of its mental attributes or of its power, or of its inner and outward value or ultimately the type of its particular existence. The 'greater' which cannot be conceived beyond the thing described is therefore quite generally: anything superior to it. And from the application which the conception is given, particularly in *Prosl. 2-4*, the definitive sense can be taken to be: the being that stands over against it as a fundamentally higher mode of being. For a fuller understanding of the literal meaning of this Name the first thing that has to be noticed is what it does not say: it does not say—God is the highest that man has in fact conceived, beyond which he can conceive nothing higher. Nor does it say—God is the highest that man could conceive. Thus it denies neither the former reality nor the latter possibility, but leaves open the question of the givenness of them both. Clearly it is deliberately chosen in such a way that the object which it describes emerges as something completely independent of whether men in actual fact conceive it or can conceive it. It is so chosen that its actual conception, as well as the possibility of its conception, emerges as being dependent upon an essentially

---

[1] So Bainvel in the *Dictionnaire de Théol. cath.*, vol. 1, Column 1351.

[2] So A. Koyré, *Saint Anselme de Cantorbéry, Fides quaerens intellectum*, Paris 1930, p. 13.

unexpressed condition.[1] All that the formula says about this object is, as far as I can see, this one thing, this one negative: nothing greater than it can be imagined; nothing can be imagined that in any respect whatsoever could or would outdo it; as soon as anyone conceives anything which in any respect whatsoever is greater than it, in so far as it can be conceived at all—then he has not yet begun to conceive it or has already ceased. It remains to be said: we are dealing with a concept of strict noetic content which Anselm describes here as a concept of God. It does not say that God is, nor what he is, but rather, in the form of a prohibition that man can understand, who he is. It is *une définition purement conceptuelle*.[2] It contains nothing in the way of statements about the existence or about the nature of the object described.[3] Thus nothing of that sort is to be derived from it on subsequent analysis. If it is to be of any use in proving the existence and nature of God then a second assumption, to be clearly distinguished from this first one, is necessary—the prior 'givenness' (credible on other grounds) of the thought of the Existence and of the Nature of God which with his help is to be raised to knowledge and proof. *Aliquid quo nihil maius cogitari possit* is therefore on no account the condensed formula of a doctrine of God that is capable of later expansion but it is a genuine description (*significatio*), one Name of God, selected from among the various revealed Names of God for this occasion and for this particular purpose, in such a way that to reach a knowledge of God the revelation of this same God from some other source is clearly assumed. All that can possibly be expected from this Name is that, in conformity with the programme of Anselm's theology, it should demonstrate that between the Name of God and the revelation of his

---

[1] It goes without saying that it immediately implies a serious misunderstanding when Wilhelm of Auxerre (died 1232) in his *Report* on Anselm's Proof thought he could interchange, that is interpret, Anselm's *cogitari* by *excogitari* (Daniels, p. 27).

[2] A. Koyré, *L'idée de Dieu, etc.*, p. 203.

[3] Again it was a crucial misunderstanding when Johannes Peckham (died 1292) quoted Anselm's Proof as the *argumentum a definitione sumptum* (Daniels, p. 44).

Existence and Nature from the other source there exists a strong and discernible connection. Only in that way and to that extent will statements about the existence and Nature of God inevitably follow from an understanding of this Name.

From what has been said we have first of all to establish that the presupposition of this Name has without any doubt a strictly theological character. Notice how the formula is introduced—*et quidem credimus te esse aliquid quo maius. . . .*[1] What is said here is confirmed by the conclusive statement in which Anselm later guarded against the possible rejection of this Name for God, that is against the fact that it is unknown to the Christian: *quod quam falsum sit, fide et conscientia tua pro firmissimo utor argumento.*[2] In this statement the *fides* of Gaunilo, who is being addressed, is itself to confirm his acquaintance with this Name of God and his *conscientia* is to confirm his acquaintance with the person whose name this is: as a believing Christian Gaunilo knows very well who the *quo maius cogitari nequit* is. With this we ought also to compare the remarkable accounts given by Anselm in the Prologue to the *Proslogion* of the discovery of this concept. He sought it *saepe studioseque,* sometimes thinking he was to find it the next moment, sometimes thinking he would never find it. Eventually he gave up the attempt as being an impossible undertaking and decided so as not to waste further time on it, not to think about it any more. As soon as he did that, however, the idea began to force itself upon him for the first time in the right way. *Cum igitur quadam die vehementer eius importunitati resistendo fatigarer, in ipso cogitationum conflictu sic se obtulit quod desperaveram, ut studiose cogitationem amplecterer, quam sollicitus repellebam.*[3] Is this a scientific report on an investigation or is it not rather a— perhaps quite typical—account of an experience of prophetic insight? However that may be: Anselm did not regard this designation for God as a non-essential theologoumenon and

---

[1] *Prosl. 2:* I 101, 4f.   [2] *C. Gaun. I:* I 130, 15f.
[3] I 93, 10ff. Compare also the *Vita* of Eadmer, *I 2, 9 (MPL* 158, 55).

certainly not as a constituent part of a universal human awareness of God,[1] but as an article of faith. If we assume for a
moment that there were for Anselm, alongside the explicit
statements of the text of the revelation, consequences arising
directly from these to which he attached equal weight,[2] then
we will have no difficulty over the fact that naturally the *quo
maius cogitari nequit* does not admit of proof by appeal to any
text that was authoritative for him.[3] Thus in no sense is he of
the opinion that he produced this formula out of his own head
but he declares quite explicitly the source from which he considers it to have come to him: when he gives God a Name, it is
not like one person forming a concept of another person; rather
it is as a creature standing before his Creator. In this relationship which is actualized by virtue of God's revelation, as he
thinks of God he knows that he is under this prohibition; he
can conceive of nothing greater, to be precise, 'better', beyond
God without lapsing into the absurdity, excluded for faith, of
placing himself above God in attempting to conceive of this
greater.[4] *Quo maius cogitari nequit* only appears to be a concept
that he formed for himself; it is in fact as far as he is concerned
a revealed Name of God.[5] Thus we see at once (how could it be

[1] This was how he was understood to a large extent later on: . . . *Anselmum,
qui dicit, quod Deus secundum communem animi conceptionem est quo nihil maius* . . .
(Bonaventura, Daniels, p. 38) . . . *arguit Anselmus . . . : Deus est secundum omnes quo
nihil maius* . . . (Joh. Peckham, Daniels, p. 43).

[2] Cf. p. 23, n. 1.

[3] In comparison we may perhaps also recall in this connection Luther's *sola fide*.

[4] *Si enim aliqua mens posset cogitare aliquid melius te, ascenderet creatura super Creatorem
et iudicaret de Creatore: quod valde est absurdum* (Prosl. 3: 1 103, 4ff). Perhaps it is not
an accident that just here as an exception Anselm brings the *melius* into use instead
of the *maius*.

[5] Among the later Scholastics who dealt with Anselm's Proof, Bonaventura and
Thomas Aquinas in particular saw correctly that what was involved in the concept
that Anselm presupposed, was the *nomen Dei* (Daniels, pp. 39 and 65f). And in
Agidius of Rome (died 1316) there is a sentence which could be the most exact
interpretation of Anselm's intention: *Demonstrare Deum esse est declarare quid est quod
importatur per hoc nomen Deus*—if Agidius did not unfortunately continue: *quod
patet ex omnibus demonstrationibus quae hoc probant* (Daniels, p. 76), from which it
follows that *nomen* in the sense of 'all' these proofs, did not mean for him the
nomen personae, but the *nomen essentiale Dei*, that is the Nature of God. And that is
how it stands with Bonaventura and Thomas as well. But the *quo maius cogitari
nequit* in Anselm himself has the meaning and plays the rôle of a *nomen personae*.

otherwise after the immediately preceding closing words of *Prosl. 1?*) that at the very outset of his Proof of the Existence of God and indeed precisely there, Anselm is fully and legitimately engaged in the exposition of his theological programme. It goes without saying that for him the Existence of God[1] is given as an article of faith. This Existence of God which is accepted in faith is now to be recognized and proved on the presupposition of the Name of God[2] likewise accepted in faith and is to be understood as necessary for thought. Thus here the Name of God is the '*a*'[3] taken from the *Credo* by means of which the Existence of God now represented as *X* is to be transformed into a known quantity from one that is unknown (not disbelieved but as yet not realized): *Nullus intelligens id quod Deus est, potest cogitare quia Deus non est.*[4] Starting from this point of the *Credo*, the other thing, the Existence of God, must make itself—not credible (it is that already)—but intelligible. The choice of this particular point, the discovery of this particular Name of God, was the first step along the path that was to commit him to the development of the Proof. That it had a vital significance for him follows just as much from the manner in which he reports his discovery in the Prologue as from the manner in which he defended it later against Gaunilo. We can be certain: at all events this first step does not lead away from the constraint of specifically theological thinking but rather leads right into it; it concerns the choice of the concrete limit which so far as this question is concerned appears to make knowledge possible.

---

[1] *Da mihi, ut . . . intelligam quia es, sicut credimus (Prosl. 2:* 1 101, 3f).

[2] Anselm's references to the revelatory-theological character of the vital assumption of his Proof are overlooked when this is understood, as is frequently done by Thomas Aquinas in particular, as an answer to the question *Utrum Deum esse sit per se notum?* There is no such *notum per se* for Anselm in theology, no insights which do not stand under the seal of faith.

[3] The Nature of God accepted by faith and already indispensable for the definition of the conception of the Existence of God certainly comes under consideration as *b*; further points of the *Credo* as *c, d, e* . . . may stand more or less visibly in the background.

[4] *Prosl. 4:* 1 103, 2of.

We are combining further comment on the Name of God which was normative for Anselm's Proof with a discussion of Gaunilo's two misunderstandings which followed immediately on this first step.

1. Gaunilo develops the thought, especially in *cap. 4-5* of his reply, that when men hear the Name of God they are unable, for lack of any kind of intuitive response and therefore of any suitable universal concept, to grasp more than a mere word (*vox*), to grasp at the same time the *rei veritas*, truth in relation to God. Whether it be the word *Deus* or Anselm's formula—the word itself could not provide him with a knowledge of God unless some extension of what the word is meant to denote were also given to him from another source. There are no less than four points here that incidentally affect Anselm.

(*a*) In his scepticism of the possibility (maintained by Anselm) of a knowledge of God, Gaunilo appears as a great champion of the concept of the incomprehensibility of God. Ought there really to be a word capable of giving knowledge of God; should any human word about God be more than a reasonably meaningful symbol of a human, an all too human, desire, that is never fulfilled, to comprehend the incomprehensible? These are the questions he feels compelled to address to Anselm. And it is quite remarkable that in so doing he felt compelled to appeal directly to Anselm.[1] Surely just a glance at *Monol. 26-27* and *64-65* would have been enough to show to anyone directing such questions to Anselm that in so doing he was merely beating the air. Also in the *Proslogion* itself he might equally well have read in the first chapter: *quia nullatenus comparo illi intellectum meum*,[2] in *cap. 15*: *Ergo Domine, non solum es quo maius cogitari nequit, sed es quiddam maius quam cogitari possit*[3] and in *cap. 16-17* a whole succession of most impressive declarations of the total hiddenness of God even for those who know him

---

[1] *Quandoquidem et tu talem asseris illam* (sc. *rem*), *ut esse non possit simile quicquam* (*Pro. insip. 4:* I 127, 2f).

[2] *Prosl. 1:* I 100, 16.   [3] *Prosl. 15:* I 112, 14f.

in faith. The only explanation for Gaunilo's obvious failure to take such passages into account is that he did not realize that for Anselm even the statement of the incomprehensibility of God was an article of faith not in any sense denied by the presupposition of the Name of God, that the whole point of the presupposition was to raise this article of faith (as well as others) to knowledge by means of the Name of God and that he indeed proved it logically in the *Proslogion* using this same Name of God.[1] How then do we know that God is incomprehensible? How do we come to assert the inadequacy of all concepts of God formed by men? Certainly for Anselm, like everything we know of the Nature of God, it follows in and by faith: in faith we are given and by faith we recognize, a designation for God which is not totally inadequate, not just a symbol, etc., for the simple reason that it expresses nothing about the nature of God but rather lays down a rule of thought which, if we follow it, enables us to endorse the statements about the Nature of God accepted in faith (example, the statement of his incomprehensibility) as our own necessary thoughts. This necessary thought which is endorsed, the Proof, itself stands of course under the shadow of the incomprehensibility of God; it stands with the proviso that thinking is merely speculative, simply *per similitudinem* not *per proprietatem*, with the proviso that in itself it is an empty shell ever requiring to be filled from above, by the Truth itself. But this proviso is also its protection: within the limits in which all theology is contained it is always true and an inviolable validity attaches to it. Against which we must seriously ask whether the incomprehensibility of God that Gaunilo so favours is anything but a statement of purely secular gnosis, not based on faith and incapable of providing any basis for a knowledge of God, and therefore whether it can really possess the critical force which it ought to have.

[1] It is proved thus: *Quoniam namque valet cogitari esse aliquid huiusmodi (sc. quiddam maius quam cogitari possit): si tu non es hoc ipsum, potest cogitari aliquid maius te: quod fieri nequit (Prosl. 15: I 112, 15ff).*

(*b*) But now Gaunilo desires and seems to regard as possible a second element of knowledge which operates in conjunction with the supposedly empty Name of God. If he had understood Anselm then he must have been aware that not even Anselm is trying with his Name of God to produce knowledge of the Nature and Existence of God out of a vacuum—a *creatio ex nihilo* indeed—but that for Anselm it is axiomatic, as the contents of the *Proslogion* indisputably show, that the element of knowledge deriving from the other source is presupposed in the articles of faith concerning the Existence and Nature of God, only that now these are treated—in respect of their knowledge-content (*not* in respect of their truth-content!)—as unknown, that is as articles that are true but still not understood. Gaunilo could not have overlooked these facts had it not been that by the second element of knowledge which he postulated he was thinking of something quite different from what Anselm was thinking. It is quite clear that when he demands an *indubium aliquod argumentum*,[1] when he wants to be sure *re vera esse alicubi maius ipsum*, in order thereby to know God's Existence by means of the concept of God,[2] when he calls for a demonstration of a *res vere atque indubie existens*,[3] the demonstration of the *esse* of that *natura maior et melior omnium*,[4] he does not mean the given-ness of an article of faith from another source which fills out the concept of God and which is to be proved by means of this concept, but quite simply he is thinking of the givenness of a corresponding idea. That this is in fact what he meant follows from the two illustrations which he himself gave of his objec-tions: when someone speaks to him about knowing 'God' he would like to know as much about 'God' from other sources as he knows at least in general from his acquaintance with other men about a particular man who may be unknown to him personally.[5] And he compares the unknown Existence of God to an unknown island in a far-off sea whose existence he will not

---

[1] *Pro insip.* 2: I 126, 9f. [2] *Ibid.* 5: I 128, 12f. [3] *Ibid.* 6: I 128, 31.
[4] *Ibid.* 7: I 129, 8f. [5] *Ibid.* 4: I 127, 4ff.

allow to be proved by a description of its perfection but only by the same method as that in which men have habitually proved the existence of hitherto unknown islands.[1] That shows how lightly he took his statement about the incomprehensibility of God. The element of knowledge other than the Name of God of which Anselm was thinking, in these circumstances must have seemed to him of little note and little comfort.

(c) For Gaunilo *quo maius cogitari nequit* is any concept as it can be formed by man with or without regard to the object concerned. Therefore he can bring into the discussion the incomprehensibility of God as an argument against the validity of knowledge in Anselm's formula. Therefore he can postulate that this formula in order to become valid for knowledge requires to be completed by an idea. For him a word in itself is in all circumstances 'only' a word, an empty word, which can however, be delivered from its emptiness where a corresponding idea is given except where the intended content is God. It is clear that from here he would only have rejected Anselm's element of knowledge from the other source and that he could also have described the article of faith about the Existence of God in respect of its epistemological validity as nothing more than an empty *vox*. That there ever could be words which even in themselves do not remain 'mere' words but are a divine revelation in the guise of something 'conceived' by a human brain in accordance with human logic and expressed in human Latin—that, in complete contrast to Anselm, was for him a totally foreign concept.

(d) In one breath Gaunilo described the *quo maius cogitari nequit* and the word *Deus* as epistemologically invalid.[2] Without giving the special content of the formula more careful consideration, he saw in *quo maius cogitari nequit* as well as in *Deus* a definition of the Perfect Nature of God which as mere *vox* was invalid. This will come out still more clearly later on. He

---

[1] *Pro insip. 6:* 1 128, 14ff.

[2] *Vix umquam poterit esse credibile, cum dictum et auditum fuerit istud, non eo modo posse cogitari non esse, quo etiam potest (cogitari) non esse Deus (Pro insip. 2:* 1 126, 4ff).

overlooked the fact that this *vox* is to be distinguished from the *vox 'Deus' aliquatenus intelligibilis*, just because its content is only of a noetic and not of an ontic nature. Anselm had of course expressly declared: *Non tento, Domine, penetrare altitudinem tuam . . . sed desidero aliquatenus intelligere veritatem tuam.*[1] Just because of the concept of God in the *Proslogion* this *aliquatenus* cannot signify a quantitative limitation of the range of human insight into the nature of God simply because this Name of God is lacking in ontic content. In that case it can only describe the noetic mediation of this Name of God. This Name of God conceives God only in that sphere in which he can be conceived,[2] not *in altitudine sua*, but with great hesitation and reserve—by conceiving the manner in which he is not to be conceived. He is not to be conceived in such a way—this possibility is ruled out by the revelation-faith relationship to him—that anything greater than him could be imagined or even imagined as conceivable. In the way of any thinker who has a hankering in this direction, the revealed Name of the Lord—his Name is *quo maius cogitari nequit*—stands as effective deterrent.[3] Since theology adheres to this command; since the noetic *ratio* of faith follows the *ratio* of the object of faith and consequently the ontic *ratio*; and since, therefore, theology assents to that Name of God as an article of faith and presupposes it for all that follows—it is able to illumine the noetic necessity of faith (that means the impossibility of denying the existence and the perfect nature of the God designated by that Name) by the roundabout route of ontic necessity which is

1 *Prosl. 1:* I 100, 15ff. *Putasne aliquatenus posse cogitari vel intelligi aut esse in cogitatione vel intellectu, de quo haec intelliguntur? (C. Gaun. 1:* I 132 3f). *Aut si aliquando negatur, quod aliquatenus intelligitur, et idem est illi quod nullatenus intelligitur: nonne facilius probatur, quod dubium est, de illo quod in aliquo, quam de eo quod in nullo est intellectu? Quare nec credibile potest esse idcirco quemlibet negare 'quo maius cogitari nequit' quod auditum aliquatenus intelligit: quia negat 'Deum', cuius sensum nullo modo cogitat. Aut si et illud, quia non omnino intelligitur, negatur: nonne tamen facilius id quod aliquo modo, quam id quod nullo modo intelligitur, probatur? (ibid. 7:* I 136, 27–137, 3).

2 *Contra insipientem ad probandum Deum esse attuli 'quo maius cogitari non possit', cum illud nullo modo, istud aliquo modo intelligeret (C. Gaun. 7:* I 137, 3ff).

3 Simply cf. *Monol. 15* (I 29, 17ff): *Nefas est putare, quod substantia supremae naturae sit aliquid, quo melius sit aliquomodo non ipsum.*

inseparable from ontic rationality. Thus theology can know what is believed, that is, prove it. In this sense, as already illustrated, the conception of God in the *Proslogion*, just because of its limitation, possesses epistemological validity. According to Anselm, to want to take *aliquatenus* as a *nullatenus* or deny validity of knowledge to this Name of God, because it does not happen to be identical with God's own conception of himself, is the same as maintaining that we cannot see the daylight because our eye in fact is not able to see the light of the sun from which the daylight proceeds.[1] He is not to be blamed for such wanton misinterpretation of this Something into Nothing.

2. Gaunilo persistently so understood Anselm's formula and in numerous passages so quoted it as if Anselm had actually written in the *Proslogion* which he was criticizing: *Aliquid, quod est maius omnibus*. We may well wonder at the gentleness with which Anselm protested[2] at this substitution and at the fact that even despite this negligence on the part of his opponent, so confusing for all concerned, he did not hesitate to acknowledge at the end of his reply Gaunilo's good-will.[3] By this negligence Gaunilo failed most seriously to appreciate that the formula which Anselm used in the *Proslogion* did not simply have a more particular content but a different content altogether from the definitions which he utilized in the *Monologion* in connection with Augustine.[4] The restlessness with which Anselm searched for a new *argumentum* in the Prologue to the *Proslogion* and the joy with which he reports having found

---

[1] *Quod si dicis, non intelligi et non esse in intellectu, quod non penitus intelligitur: dic quia qui non potest intueri purissimam lucem solis, non videt lucem diei, quae non est nisi ux solis* (C. Gaun. *1:* I 132, 5ff).

[2] *Nusquam in omnibus dictis meis invenitur talis probatio . . . iniuste me reprehendisti dixisse quod non dixi* (C. Gaun. *5:* I 134, 26f; 135, 22f). By *omnia dicta* the *Proslogion* is primarily intended, to which alone Gaunilo was referring. The *Monologion* can, however, be intended as well in so far as there too the *maius omnibus* is not applied to the Proof of the Existence of God.

[3] *benevolentia* (C. Gaun. *10:* I 139, 11).

[4] The conception of God in the *Monologion* which Gaunilo was obviously listening to, meant: the greatest or highest or best: *aliquid maximum et optimum id est summum omnium quae sunt* (Monol. *2:* I 15, 22f). *Necesse est, ut sit (sc. substantia supremae naturae) quidquid omnino melius est, quam non ipsum* (ibid. *15:* I 29, 19). God is *aliqua*

it could not be explained had he been able to accept one of these older definitions as equivalent to his new *argumentum*. In the same passage he declared what the new *argumentum* that he was seeking ought to achieve: namely, it ought to be sufficient as *unum argumentum* to prove the Existence and Nature of God.[1] And certainly it ought to have such force of proof that in its structure it may correspond to what faith holds to be the Nature of God and therefore be able to be used to prove God in a manner befitting God. Thus God's Nature is soon transcribed as follows: God alone is the *summum bonum nullo alio indigens et quo omnia indigent ut sint et bene sint.* That, however, means that the Name of God on the presupposition of which the Existence and Nature of this God are to be proved, must be so formed that in view of the Existence of God believed but not proved, or Nature of God believed but not proved,[2] it is enough to conceive this Name or express it, in order thereby to complete the required proof.[3] The formula corresponding to Anselm's previous position, which was carelessly drawn into the

substantia quam censet (sc. homo) supra omnem naturam, quae Deus non est (ibid. 80: I 86, 20f). That is in fact, though not literally, Gaunilo's '*quod est maius omnibus*'. Cf. in this respect, Augustine's: *(Deus) ita cogitatur, ut aliquid quo nihil melius sit atque sublimius illa cogitatio conetur attingere* . . . Thus God is the Greatest that can be imagined—perhaps this was the passage that formed the starting-point from which Anselm aspired to his later formula, which is also characteristically different from this Augustinian one . . . *nec inveniri potest, qui hoc Deum credat esse, quo melius aliquid est (De doctr. chr. I 7).* We may notice how in this second sentence Augustine again moved away from the direction in which Anselm proceeded further. So also in this second passage which belongs to it: *Hunc plane fatebor Deum, quo nihil superius esse constiterit (De lib. arb. II 6, 14).* We can see Anselm's whole relation to Augustine at this point condensed in the passage *C. Gaun. 10* (I 139, 3ff): *credimus namque de divina substantia quidquid absolute cogitari potest melius esse quam non esse.* (Anselm goes so far with Augustine) . . . *Nihil autem huiusmodi non esse potest, quo maius aliquid cogitari non potest. Necesse igitur est 'quo maius cogitari non potest' esse, quidquid de divina essentia credi oportet.* (Here we are dealing with thoughts of Anselm's that are independent of Augustine.)

[1] *Prosl. Prologue:* I 93, 6ff. He calls the *Monologion,* by way of a reproach *multorum concatenatione contextum argumentorum (ibid.:* I 93, 5), and with this is obviously objecting that there the Name of God as such has none at all of the systematic significance which he now wants to give it.

[2] The prior-givenness of a subject of the Proof can naturally not be excluded by the 'aseity' of the Name presupposed.

[3] *Argumentum, quod nullo alio ad se probandum quam se solo indigeret (Prosl. Prologue:* I 93, 6f). *In isto vero (sc. argumento) non est opus alio quam hoc ipso quod sonat: quo maius cogitari non possit.* . . . *de se per seipsum probat 'quo maius nequit cogitari' (C. Gaun. 5:* I 135, 19ff; cf. also *ibid. 10:* I 138, 30ff).

discussion by Gaunilo,—*quod est maius omnibus*—would not conform to these conditions. This can be seen at once to be simply a transliteration back into ontic terminology of the noetic terminology which Anselm is now deliberately choosing and to which he is careful to give point. Neither is it in the narrow, strict sense a designation or Name of God like *quo maius cogitari nequit*, but in itself it is a brief paraphrase of the Nature of God. As such, therefore as far as proof is concerned alike both of the Existence and Nature of God as these are held by faith, it is insufficient. It is no accident that though in various passages[1] in the *Monologion* Anselm asserts the Existence of God as held by faith, he did not try to prove it. The insight that such proof is impossible on the basis of the conception of God assumed in the *Monologion*, is perhaps a later achievement. It comes to formal expression in the answer to Gaunilo[2] and is based on the fact that *quod est maius omnibus* might also be conceived of as not-existing. As long, however, as the conception that is presupposed does not in itself rule out that possibility and as long, therefore, as the non-existence of God is conceivable without the presupposed conception of God being destroyed, this conception is not amenable to proof because a proof of the Existence of God is only being discussed when this Existence is demonstrated as necessary to thought (that is, as impossible not to be thought). But in the same context Anselm also declares—and that by way of public self-correction apropos the *Monologion*—that that conception would not be sufficient to prove what faith holds to be the Nature of God and for the reason that once again *quod est maius omnibus* does not preclude the possibility that a *maius eo (etiam si non sit)* could at least be conceived.[3] However, even the exclusion of such a possibility

---

[1] Explicit *Monol. 6*; implicit *ibid. 31* and *34*.   [2] *C. Gaun. 5:* I 134, 27ff.

[3] *Quid enim: si quis dicat esse aliquid maius omnibus quae sunt et idipsum tamen posse cogitari non esse et aliquid maius eo etiam si non sit posse tamen cogitari? An hic sic aperte inferri potest: non est ergo maius omnibus quae sunt . . . ? (C. Gaun. 5:* I 135, 14ff). Not only in the *Proslogion* but also in the later work *De veritate*, where once again Anselm gave a Proof of the Nature of God (*De verit. 1:* I 176, 12), we see him as a result working with the *impossibile est cogitare. . . .*

would have to be accomplished by a real proof of the originally perfect Nature of God. Obviously Gaunilo could not have attempted anything more devastating than his ill-considered re-transliteration into ontic terms of the new formula that Anselm introduced in the *Proslogion*. The very thing that Anselm intended should make it valid as a proof, its austere character as a rule for thinking about God, was thereby taken away from it and it is hardly surprising that, on the basis of this presupposition, Gaunilo was not able to appreciate Anselm's actual Proof. Again, he is just beating the air when he thinks it necessary to inform Anselm that by means of this conception the Proof is not possible.[1]

The invalidity for proof which Anselm himself asserted of the *quod est maius omnibus* stood in very close connection with a second consideration, namely that as a Name of God it did not possess that self-sufficiency that belongs to and befits the nature of its subject. For the *quod est maius omnibus* to become admissible as proof, it required certain presuppositions not contained within itself. That is, in order to be the highest, it must first presuppose the existence and nature of *omnia*, that is of objects which in their existence and nature point beyond themselves to the 'highest' which forms their peak. Without the rest of the pyramid the peak could not be a peak. *De minoribus bonis ad maiora conscendendo* (as Anselm described it, still in his reply to Gaunilo) do we arrive at the conception of the *optimum maximum summum*. It is only from other heights that the highest comes into view. From the existence and nature of the lower we may *conicere*, form tentative conclusions about, such a highest: the unbeliever is to be reminded that we can do this and the believer is to be reminded from Rom. 1.20 that our ability to do this is a truth of revelation.[2] But—in so doing

---

[1] The fact that Anselm's Proof became known in wider theological circles during the thirteenth century was in the end unfortunate. The first to take it up (Richard Fishacre, Wilhelm of Auxerre, Alexander of Hales, cf. Daniels, pp. 24, 27, 30f) immediately compromised it by introducing it within a series of proofs of God clearly based on ontic assumptions each and all of which Anselm had declared to be ambiguous. [2] *C. Gaun. 8:* 1 137, 18 and 27ff.

neither the nature nor even the existence of the 'highest' as such is known or proved. For why should it not be conceived of as not existing, or, if existing, capable of being surpassed?[1]

In order to be valid for proof the conception of the 'highest' requires in the second place to be supplemented by such another concept as excludes the very possibility of this mode of thinking. This vital concept is just the *quo maius cogitari nequit*. In so far as the *maius omnibus* is thought of as identical to the *quo maius cogitari nequit*, the existence and perfection of what it describes can be proved—but not otherwise.[2] Therefore it has none of that self-sufficiency with which it would correspond to its object. This self-sufficiency does, however, belong to the Name of God discovered in the *Proslogion*. The designation of God as the *quo maius cogitari nequit* does not assume the existence or nature of any creature, certainly not of God himself, neither as actually conceived nor as being conceivable. It simply says that if God should or could be conceived—that both these are in fact so is obviously the other assumption, the substance of the Proof—then nothing else may be conceived of as greater than God. For all its formal, or noetic insufficiency it stands on its own feet. The Proof that is to be worked out on the assump-

---

[1] It is just in *C. Gaun. 8*, where the inherent continuity between Anselm's new formula and the conception of God in the *Monologion* comes out most clearly, that he lays great emphasis on the fact that the question *sive sit in re aliquid huiusmodi, sive non sit* cannot be answered along the road taken in the *Monologion* (*via eminentiae*).

[2] From this standpoint too Gaunilo's island analogy is shown up as a useless notion. Gaunilo takes the *quo maius cogitari nequit* as a definition of the Nature of God and Anselm's Proof as deriving God's Existence from God's Nature as that is thus established. In actual fact for Anselm the Proof of the Nature of God follows just as much as the Proof of his Existence from the *quo maius cogitari nequit*, and indeed in such a way that the latter is prior to the former. Anselm too does not think first of the perfection of that 'island' in order to know its existence; Anselm also wants to know first of all its existence but most certainly from a less unreliable source than the general experience of which Gaunilo is clearly thinking. And to that extent he wants to know of its perfection too, then of its unique perfection that is not to be confused with any other: *Nullatenus enim potest intelligi 'quo maius cogitari non possit', nisi id, quod solum omnibus est maius. Sicut ergo 'quo maius cogitari nequit' intelligitur et est in intellectu, et ideo esse in rei veritate asseritur: sic quod maius dicitur omnibus, intelligi et esse in intellectu et idcirco re ipsa esse ex necessitate concluditur. Vides ergo quam recte me comparasti stulto illi qui hoc solo, quod descripta intelligeretur, perditam insulam vellet asserere?* (*C. Gaun. 5*: I 135, 26ff).

tion of this designation of God will not be an analytic but a synthetic proposition.[1] In that it corresponds to its object.[2] And likewise it can now be valid as a proof: it is able to perform the same function as the presupposed Name of God is to perform in a Proof of God. With *quo maius cogitari nequit* the enemy (denial or doubt) is sought out on his own ground, in thought itself, on which ground this enemy is repeatedly calling in question the knowledge of God on the assumption of an ontic conception of God, and is placed under the sign of the Name of God and is thereby challenged to necessary knowledge of God. *Quo maius cogitari nequit* is designed to exclude just this conceivability of the non-existence or imperfection of God which lurks in the background of every ontic conception of God— to exclude it with the radicalism and force of the Creator's own injunction to the creature—*non eritis sicut Deus*—and likewise to establish knowledge of the truth of the existence and perfection of God.

We may say that the motive that led Anselm to choose this particular Name was completely misunderstood by Gaunilo. Otherwise the *maius omnibus* would not have appeared at all. Our understanding of Anselm's intention will depend on our avoiding right from the start this erroneous substitution by Gaunilo.[3]

2. THE QUESTION OF THE EXISTENCE OF GOD

It is part of the advance which the *Proslogion* represents on the *Monologion* that now the question of the Existence of God (*quia es*) stands out as a special problem distinct from the

[1] Above all the *argumentum* proves itself, as it stated in the passages quoted in note 3 on page 85 and therefore it may also be used as a means of proof.

[2] Cf. with this the older statement on the aseity of God: *Si enim nulla earum rerum umquam esset, quarum relatione summa et maior dicitur, ipsa nec summa nec maior intelligretur: nec tamen idcirco minus bona esset aut essentialis suae magnitudinis in aliquo detrimentum pateretur* (*Monol. 15:* 1 13ff).

[3] How remarkable it is that even so clever and independent an historian as F. Overbeck (*op. cit.*, p. 220) could not rise even a little above the level of the common but false explanation of the basic concept of our Proof.

problem of the Nature of God (*quia hoc es*). Naturally, even in the *Monologion* Anselm is acquainted with the concept *esse* in the sense of *existere* or *subsistere*;[1] just as even there he had also asserted the Existence of God to be an article of faith. But it belongs to the powers which are there assumed to be known and at that point perhaps Anselm did not even think of it as a possible problem, as the *X* to be solved. At least it was not till the *Proslogion* that it became for him the object of *intellectus fidei*, that is of the Proof, in a way that may be thus distinguished: that now he broaches the question of *esse* right at the beginning of the book as prior to the question of the Nature of God.

In the *Monologion* the meaning of the concept 'existence' is clarified once we see that the three phrases *essentia, esse existens sive subsistens* are compared with one another and it is said of them that they are inter-related as *lux, lucere* and *lucens*.[2] In view of Anselm's later statements, which will be quoted later, we may venture the following interpretation: *essentia* meants potentiality (*potentia*), *esse* the reality (*actus*) of an object's existence. But it is called *existens sive subsistens* in so far as it exists, that is—it is best to keep to the negative definition— in so far as it is an object not just in human thinking or for human thinking. *Essentia* and *esse* may also belong to an object in such a way that its existence is presupposed in an act of human thinking—for in so far as it is conceived, it is conceived as existing. However, it is still not settled whether this act of thinking has in relation to the presupposition the character of mere hypothesis, fiction, lie or mistake. All that would mean: the object concerned exists only as presupposition of this act of thinking, therefore it possesses no existence. However, this amounts to: it does not exist, though it may be that statements logical and meaningful in themselves can be made about the

---

[1] For example, *Monol. 6:* I 19, 21f; *ibid. 16:* I 30, 22ff; *ibid. 28:* I 45, 25ff; *ibid. 31:* I 49, 3f; *ibid. 34:* I 53, 17f.

[2] *Monol. 6:* I 20, 15ff.

potentiality and reality of its nature (for instance, about the abilities and deeds of a fictitious character). On the other hand, the description *ex-sistens* or *sub-sistens* applied to an object characterizes it simultaneously as emerging (*ex-sistens*) from the inner circle of abstract existence (where it also exists in so far as it forms the subject of discussion), as 'existing for itself' as opposed to all thinking of the potentiality or reality of its existence as well as of its actual existence, existing (*sub-sistens*) independently (even when not debarred from our thinking); existence belongs to it, it exists, although perhaps very little or nothing at all may be stated about the potentiality or reality of its existence. This interpretation of the *Monologion* passage will be illuminating if we place alongside it what we hear in the *Proslogion* and in the Answer to Gaunilo about the concept of Existence. Here on one occasion Anselm makes this distinction: it is *aliud rem esse in intellectu, aliud intelligere rem esse.* The first *esse* may imply the non-existence of the *res* apart from its existence in thought, as, for instance, the *esse* of a picture *in intellectu* of the artist before the completion of the actual work. The second *esse* is the existence of the *res* apart from its existence in thought which is added to the first *esse*, as, for instance, the *esse* of the picture when the artist's work is finished: *et habet in intellectu et intelliget esse.*[1] A second distinction goes even deeper (by a different application this time of the term *res*): an object either has *esse in intellectu solo* or *esse et in intellectu et in re.*[2] On the one hand, potentiality of being and reality of being as determining an object which on occasion exists merely in thought, and, on the other hand, actual existence are clearly related to one another,[3] according to Anselm, as an inner circle is related to an outer one: when an object is thought of as having potentiality of existence and

---

[1] *Prosl. 2:* I 101, 10ff.

[2] *Prosl. 2:* I 102, 3; *C. Gaun. 2:* I 132, 22f; *ibid. 6:* I 136, 7f.

[3] He certainly did not want by this to exclude and could not exclude the further possible case of an *esse in re sola* (God 'before' the Creation); but this did not come into the question of knowledge.

reality of existence it is also thought of as existing, be that mere hypothesis, poetic licence, deception or error. But the fact that existence does belong to it, that it is not merely thought to be existing, that its existence is neither hypothesis nor poetry, neither deceit nor mistake—is not contained in the thought of its power to exist or of the reality of its existence. That has to be —and this assumption comes into the discussion independently—specially thought, and if known and proved then it has to be specially known and proved.

The question of this special thought and proof is the question of existence. It is distinguished from all other questions of knowledge as the question of the object of knowledge, of the object as such and to what extent it is not merely what we *think*, but *what* we think. It asks whether and to what extent this object, as surely as it is the object of thought, at the same time stands over against thought and is itself not to be reduced to something that is merely thought; it asks whether and to what extent, while belonging to the inner circle of what is thought, it also 'protrudes' into the outer circle of what is not only thought, but exists independently of thought. For Anselm, on this *ex-sistere* of the object depends nothing less than its Trueness. Its being in truth is for Anselm, as it were, the third and last outer circle by which the existence and within the existence, the existence in thought, must be enclosed if a thought, that is an object that is thought, is to be true. The object then is first of all in reality, then following from that it exists, then as a consequence of that it can be thought. Without the middle step of existing what is thought could not be real. Anything really *in intellectu solo* (that is excluding the *esse in re*) would be *falsum*; on the other hand what is *et in intellectu et in re* is identical with what is real[1] because it could not be *in re* had it not first existed in reality. As we heard earlier, the truth of a statement depends precisely on this: that it describes as existing something in fact existing.[2] The question of the

[1] *C. Gaun. 6:* I 136, 7f.   [2] *De verit. 2:* I 178, 6f; cf. p. 46, n. 2.

knowledge of an object must go further than knowing it as existing (that means, in knowing it as having power and reality of existence). To be true knowledge, to be knowledge of the truth, it must press on to knowledge of the existence of the object thus known in itself, to knowledge of its objectivity. Not till the question of knowledge reaches this second outer circle, not till it probes whether the object exists beyond mere thought, is it really in earnest. Not till then does it press into the third or inclusive realm of truth. However, once the urgency of the question of existence is seen as a question of truth, everything will depend on grasping it and answering it in its special nature. It cannot be confused again with the question of the power and reality of the existence, the potentiality and actuality, the *essentia* and *esse* of the object. Furthermore, the appearance must be avoided that it is a case of elevating existence in thought analytically to actual existence. It must be clear that the question of existence, far from being involved in the question of nature, is an entirely new question. That the question of nature is thereby assumed to be answered—whose existence is being questioned must of course be fixed—is another matter. But the existence may not be derived from the nature of the object whose existence is in question. The question of existence must quite definitely be asked on the assumption that in no sense whatsoever is it answered along with the question of nature.[1] Obviously in this last respect Anselm did not only sever the question of existence from that of nature in the *Proslogion* but gave it priority of study.

The doctrine of the Nature of God which comes up for discussion in the *Monologion* and in *Prosl. 5-26* deals with God's *essentia* and *esse* and *in nuce* declares that in distinction to all

---

[1] Bonaventura and, following him, Matthew of Aquasparta, raised the objection against Gaunilo's island analogy (*Pro insip. 6*) that the description of the island as perfect means an *oppositio in adiecto* which is not the case when the same description is applied to God (Daniels, pp. 40 and 62). The objection is valid and therefore represents a compromise on Anselm's part in so far as he had to confirm the impression that Gaunilo's task was to conclude the Existence of God from a correctly worked out conception of his nature.

other creative beings these two in God are not two, but one. By virtue of his aseity, or his glory as Creator, God is all that he is, not through participation in certain potentialities not identical with his actual Power; all his potentialities do not first require to be actualized in the reality of his Power, but he is himself what he ever is and what he ever is, he is himself. His Potentiality and his Reality are identical.[1] The proof of this potential Reality or actualized Potentiality of God had been worked out in the *Monologion* on the assumption of the *maius omnibus* as the conception of God and with the question of the Existence of God left open. We saw how in the *Proslogion* Anselm came to substitute for that conception of God the *quo maius cogitari nequit* and thereby to prove even the Nature of God in a different way. Obviously with this he was disturbed by the proximity of that open question to the other part of his Doctrine of God.[2] Of course, for faith the Existence of God is not an open question. There is naturally not the slightest suspicion that the Existence of God, as an article of faith, might just be hypothesis, fiction, deceit or error. But to see the impossibility of conceiving the non-existence of God is not the same as the certainty with which faith conceives the existence of God. Inability to see this must seem to threaten the knowledge of God's Nature already gained. Here too the required knowledge of faith cannot rest content with an unsolved X. It has to be shown that it is impossible to conceive the object described as God as being only a conception. To show

---

[1] *Quidquid . . . de illa (sc. summa essentia) dicatur: non qualis vel quanta, sed magis quid sit monstratur (Monol. 16:* I 31, 1f). *Idem igitur est quodlibet unum eorum* (of the divine attributes) *quod omnia, sive simul sive singula (ibid. 17:* I 31, 23f). *Tu vero es, quod es, qvia quidquid aliquando aut aliquo modo es, hoc totus et semper es (Prosl. 22:* I 116, 20f). *Summa veritas . . . nulli quicquam debet; nec ulla ratione est quod est, nisi quia est (De verit. 10:* I 190, 4). *Non tibi est aliud essentia quam bonitas et omnipotentia . . . et omnia illa quae similiter de te dicuntur et creduntur (Medit. 19, 3: MPL* 158, 805).

[2] The first possible meaning of the title of *Prosl. 2* (I 101, 2): *quod vere sit Deus* is therefore this: the question of truth in regard to God's existence is to be taken seriously in such a way that the question advances beyond the 'inner' circle of the mere thought of the object into the 'outer' circle of the thought of this particular object as such—and so it advances in the direction of truth itself.

this is the purpose of the Proof of the Existence of God in *Prosl.* 2-4.

But for all that we have so far said, we have still not fully brought out the specific and characteristic urgency which constrained Anselm to prove the Existence of God.

Our exposition to this point could even be used in support of an ancient misunderstanding. Because of our synoptic view we have done what Anselm himself did not do and have spoken first of the question of the existence of objects in general and then of the question of the Existence of God. This is liable to cause misunderstanding for it suggests that the question of the Existence of God is to be understood as a special case of the general question of the existence of any object and is to be answered accordingly. And the originator of this misunderstanding too is Gaunilo. Just as he deemed the concept of God to be a general concept so he took the Existence of God to be existence in general. By so doing he misconstrued Anselm's second step just as he did the first, and of course the immediate consequence is that for him the question of the Existence of God is nothing like as urgent as it is for Anselm.

The fact that Gaunilo is able to speak of the Existence of God and of the unknown island in the sea in one and the same breath highlights two things: the whittling down of the special question of the Existence of God to the level of the general question of existence, and the consequent merging and begging of that special question.[1] It is clear that the Proof of the Existence of the Island is fundamentally different from the Proof of God's Existence and that the form of proof, however desirable it might be, can if necessary be entirely dispensed with because there is no question at all of there being an ultimate necessity to conceive the existence of this particular island. But for

[1] We can but cast the mantle of charity over the fact that in this context later participants in the discussion even spoke of the winged horse Pegasus and of—'a hundred dollars'!

Gaunilo it is exactly the same with the Proof of God. The passion with which Anselm wants to know the Existence of God because he believes it and therefore must think it, is quite foreign to Gaunilo. For Gaunilo it might equally well remain unproved. His curious passion is reserved on the other hand for asserting that it might very well be possible to conceive of God as existing only as a conception.[1] The entire apologia *Pro Insipiente* is in support of this freedom. It gives no indication itself of having any kind of grasp of the problem or of any concern to find a better solution than Anselm's which it rejected. Certainly Gaunilo is an eager thinker, keen and honest, but the only pressure he feels is the pressure to avoid Anselm's position in his fierce criticism of Anselm's solution. Is he not sure of his faith? Or, is he quite unaware of a *fides quaerens intellectum*? He has been described as a sceptic, as a traditionalist, and it may be that perhaps he was both. What is certain is that his feverish activity in this matter is not reflected in his knowledge of his argument. He must not conceive the Existence of God. All his passion confirms the impression that he really must not do that. Therefore he cannot wish to prove it. Free from this twofold compulsion and in the guise of a non-partisan seeker after truth, he has sufficient time and leisure to treat himself to the fun of a *Liber pro insipiente*. He was neither the first nor the last 'theologian' of that breed.

Anselm's constraint at the outset of his Proof is best illustrated by his classic reply to Gaunilo's remarks concerning the lost island: he confidently asserts that he can once and for all prove the existence of this island if anyone is in a position to convince him of the existence or even just the concept of something, which though different from what is described by his Name of God, yet might reasonably be the subject of the same proof.[2] Now that means: Anselm proves the existence of

---

[1] *Pro insip. 2:* I 125, 14ff; *ibid. 7:* I 129, 14.

[2] *Fidens loquor, quia si quis invenerit mihi aut re ipsa aut sola cogitatione existens praeter 'quo maius cogitari non possit', cui aptare valeat conexionem huius meae argumentationis: inveniam et dabo illi perditam insulam amplius non perdendam (C. Gaun. 3:* I 133, 6ff).

a thing when it is existence alone that can be proved.[1] Under the pressure thus exerted the proof of the Existence of God is for him a demand.

We saw: the fact that God exists cannot be derived from his Nature; for over against all answers to the question—'What is God?'—the question—'Is there a God?'—remains a special, open question (albeit closed as far as certainty of faith is concerned). The conception of God then that is presupposed in a proof of the Existence of God must not therefore be a kind of disguised doctrine of his Nature. We may certainly make inferences from the Nature of God as to what existence in general can and does mean, but it is for God to say how far we are right or wrong. The real meaning of Existence as attributed to God, even if attributed only in thought, has to be investigated always with the question left open—this is what has to be proved—whether it is impossible to conceive of God as existing only as a concept. Existence means in general the existence of an object without regard to whether it is thought of as existing. The reality of an object and the fact of its being thought of demand that it exists. But even the reality by itself demands both its existence and true thinking of its existence. It exists and is rightly thought of as existing because and to the extent that it is first of all real. The decision as to whether it exists and whether it is truly conceived is not made in and by itself but is made within the third all-inclusive circle, that is on the basis of Truth itself. This decisive Truth is God. And it is his Existence that is involved. It is certainly also true that the point at issue

---

[1] *Proprium est Deo, non posse intelligi non esse.* For: *illa quippe omnia et sola possunt cogitari non esse, quae initium aut finem aut partium habent coniunctionem et . . . quidquid alicubi aut aliquando totum non est. Illud vero solum non potest cogitari non esse, in quo nec initium nec finem nec partium coniunctionem, et quod non nisi semper et ubique totum ulla invenit cogitatio* (*ibid. 4:* I 133, 27f; 134, 2ff). Bonaventura was wrong when he thought that there was a further proof by Anselm of the Existence of God to be found in this passage (Daniels, p. 39). Anselm's point in *cap. 4* of his essay against Gaunilo is not a proof of the Existence of God but a proof of the fact that in the strict sense which Anselm means the only thing that can be proved is the Existence of God. This subsidiary proof is worked out from the Nature of God, where it belongs. But just for that reason it cannot serve and it cannot be meant as a proof of the Existence of God.

here is existence plain and simple: the Existence of God apart from his Existence in thought. But because God is Truth what is meant is obviously existence in a superlative sense, not the *existere* of objects that is conditioned by truth in the second or middle circle, but the *existere* of Truth itself which is the condition, the basis and indeed the fashioner of all other existence, the simple origin of all objectivity, of all true outward being and therefore also of all true inner being. God exists—if he does exist—in the unique manner that befits him as the only One who ultimately really exists.[1] What is outside of him has its existence by his grace,[2] is created by him out of nothing[3] and is also kept from complete disintegration only by the same gracious-creative activity of God.[4] Apart therefore from the will and work of God all that is not God would not exist. Thus all that is not God exists, so to say, enclosed within the purpose of God's conceiving.[5] In itself and from itself at no point had it the possibility of existence but only from God and from God alone.[6] It obtains existence by the Word of God.[7]

---

[1] *Iste spiritus, qui sic suo quodam mirabiliter singulari et singulariter mirabili modo est, quadam ratione solus est, alia vero quaecumque videntur esse, huic collata, non sunt* (Monol. *28:* I 45, 25ff). *Secundum hanc igitur rationem solus ille creator spiritus est, et omnia creata non sunt* (ibid. *28:* I 46, 29f). *Solus igitur verissime omnium et ideo maxime omnium habes esse, quia quidquid aliud est, non sic vere, et idcirco minus habet esse* (Prosl. *3:* I 103 7ff). *Quid es nisi . . . summum omnium solum existens per seipsum* (Prosl. *5:* I 104, 11f). *Ille itaque, cuius esse tam excellens, tam singulariter est, ut solum vere sit, in cuius comparatione omne esse nihil est . . .* (Medit. *1, 3: MPL* 158, 712). *Tu vero vere es, et non est aliud nisi tu* (ibid. *19, 3: MPL* 158, 805).

[2] *Omnis enim creatura gratia existit, quia gratia facta est* (De concordia Qu. III *2:* II 264, 18).

[3] *Illa summa essentia tantam rerum molem . . . sola per seipsam, produxit ex nihilo* (Monol. *7:* I 22, 7ff).

[4] *non solum non est aliqua alia essentia nisi illo faciente, sed nec aliquatenus manere potest quod facta est nisi eodem ipso servante* (De casu diab. *1:* I 234, 19ff). *Necesse est ut, sicut nihil factum est nisi per creatricem praesentem essentiam, ita nihil vigeat nisi per eiusdem servatricem praesentiam* (Monol. *13:* I 27, 13ff). *Quidquid aliud est, ne in nihilum cadat, ab ea praesente sustinetur* (ibid. *22:* I 41, 6f; cf. ibid. *28:* I 46, 17f).

[5] *Non nihil erant* (sc. ante creationem) *quantum ad rationem facientis, per quam et secundum quam fierent* (Monol. *9:* I 24, 19f).

[6] *Omnino nihil potuit* (sc. mundus) *antequam esset. . . . Non ergo potuit esse antequam esset . . . Sed Deo, in cuius potestate erat ut fieret, erat possibile. Quia ergo Deus prius potuit facere mundum quam fieret, ideo est mundus non quia ipse mundus potuit prius esse* (De casu diab. *12:* I 253, 9ff).

[7] *Summam substantiam constat prius in se quasi dixisse cunctam creaturam, quam eam secundum eandem et per eandem suam intimam locutionem conderet* (Monol. *11:* I 26, 3ff).

And also it has no existence other than that which it has in the Word of God; in so far as it is, and what it is, it is in the Word and by the Word.[1] And for that very reason in the end it can certainly be known to exist in the usual way, but it cannot be proved to exist.[2] In this way therefore the Existence of God of which Anselm speaks and which he wants to prove, is distinguished from all other existence.

The *Monologion* had closed with these words, which can only be understood in this context: *Vere igitur hic est non solum Deus sed solus Deus ineffabiliter trinus et unus.*[3] To prove that this One to whom none may be likened has unique existence and alone has existence that can be proved, is clearly a task whose urgency is beyond all comparison with other existence proofs. The proof of this particular existence is not demanded because the knowledge that God exists in the same way as everything else exists would be indispensable for a knowledge of the Truth of God. Of course he exists in this way also but he does not exist only or primarily in this way. If he did exist solely and primarily in this way then the Proof of his Existence would be as desirable, but also as dispensable, as every other existence proof. The Existence of God is not only unique but it is the sole existence which is real and ultimate, the very basis of all other existences and therefore just because of that also the only existence which in the strict sense can be proved. Also while he does exist in the same way as everything else exists, in reality he exists first and foremost in the manner peculiar to himself. Supposing that his Existence to thought were of necessity

---

[1] *Existendi veritas intelligatur in verbo* (*Monol. 31:* I 49, 3). *Cum ipse summus spiritus dicit seipsum, dicit omnia, quae facta sunt. Nam et antequam fierent et cum iam facta sunt et cum corrumpuntur seu aliquo modo variantur: semper in ipso sunt, non quod sunt in seipsis, sed quod est idem ipse. Etenim in seipsis sunt essentia mutabilis secundum immutabilem rationem creata, in ipso vero sunt ipsa prima essentia* (the Being) *et prima existendi veritas* (*ibid. 34:* I 53, 21ff). *An putas aliquid esse aliquando aut alicubi, quod non sit in summa veritate, et quod inde non acceperit quod est inquantum est, aut quod possit aliud esse quam quod ibi est? . . . Absolute concludere potes quia omne quod est, vere est, quoniam non est aliud quam quod ibi est* (*De verit. 7:* I 185, 11ff).

[2] *Quidquid est . . . etiam cum scitur esse, posse non esse cogitari* (*C. Gaun. 4:* I 134, 15f).

[3] *Monol. 80:* I 87, 12f.

propounded by faith in God, it would still have to be known and proved: not only because the knowledge of all other existences (just the opposite of what Gaunilo thinks) stands or falls with the knowledge of this Existence, but because here and only here the question of Existence itself is being raised and not just (again as Gaunilo thinks) the question of the existence of any particular thing. The question of this Existence must be raised just as surely as the question of truth has to be raised.[1] It is possible for us to avoid the question of the existence of this or that particular thing. No thing exists so necessarily that knowledge of it is indispensable because no thing has real, ultimate existence. God is the object of knowledge who has absolute necessity as the One who does exist. If he is surrendered to thought by his revelation in faith then there will be no dispensing with the necessity to prove this thing that is believed.

B. The Development of the Proof
Commentary on *Prosl.* 2-4

1. THE GENERAL EXISTENCE OF GOD (*Prosl.* 2)

From the findings of source criticism we may assume[2] that the chapter headings in the *Proslogion* go back to Anselm himself. The title of *Prosl.* 2 runs:

Quod vere sit Deus (1 101, 2)   That God truly exists.

In this whole context *esse* is to be translated as *existere*: *Prosl.* 2-4, apart from the first lines of introduction, deals with the question of the Existence of God. The beginning of *Prosl.* 5: *Quid igitur es . . .?* introduces the second problem of the book,

---

[1] The second possible meaning of the title of *Prosl.* 2: *Quod vere sit Deus* is as follows: that existent must be sought which, in so far as it exists uniquely in truth, is itself the basis of all existence.

[2] This is also suggested by the last lines of the *Praefatio* to *Cur Deus homo* (II 43, 4ff).

that of the Nature of God. The adverb *vere* has two meanings with reference to the problem of the divine *esse*, that is *existere*. 1. It refers to God's existence generally. God does not exist only in thought but over against thought. Just because he exists not only 'inwardly' but also 'outwardly' (*in intellectu et in re*), he (from the human standpoint) 'truly' exists, exists from the side of truth and therefore really exists. 2. It refers to the existence that is utterly unique to God. God does not only exist in the manner of other existents (over against thinking, independent, in true objectivity). But God exists in the uniquely true manner that befits the Existent One who is at once the Origin and Basis of all that exists apart from him and beside him—and therefore the Origin and Basis of all reality behind the conception of any existence. *Prosl. 2* proves the existence of God in the first possible sense of the *vere esse* and *Prosl. 3* in the second sense. *Prosl. 4* illustrates the fact of the antithesis—'there is no God'. *Quod vere sit Deus* might therefore suggest in itself the contents of *Prosl. 2* and *3*. As Anselm gave the special theme of *Prosl. 3* its own title, we may assume that with the title of *Prosl. 2* what he had in mind was the first sense of *vere esse* corresponding to the contents of this chapter: the first point that is at issue here is the existence of God in general, that he exists at all.

Ergo Domine, qui das fidei intellectum, da mihi, ut quantum scis expedire, intelligam quia es sicut credimus, et hoc es quod credimus. (1 101, 3f)	Therefore, Lord, who givest knowledge to faith, grant in whatever measure thou willest, that I may know that thou dost exist as we believe and that thou art what we believe.

As we said earlier: Anselm thinks and proves in prayer and therefore not on logical presuppositions but by acceptance in practice of the existence of the One whose existence he undertakes to think out and prove. The point of the proof which is becoming visible in *Prosl. 3* would be missed, and so the whole thing misunderstood, were the fact to be ignored that Anselm speaks about God while speaking to him. The knowledge which the proof seeks to expound and impart is the knowledge that is peculiar to faith, knowledge of what is believed from what is believed. It is—and this is why it has to be sought in prayer—a knowledge that must be bestowed on man. The condition *quantum scis expedire* is related to *aliquatenus intelligere* at the end of *Prosl. 1*, and asserts primarily that the scientific experiment about to be undertaken will take place within the limits which God himself imposes on noetic investigation. There can be no question of exploring the divine *altitudo*. From this point the references go on to agree that the measure of clarity and distinctness with which the seeker is able to view such knowledge at any particular moment of history (in relation to those who have gone before and who will come after), is a matter of Divine Providence. The *Proslogion* as a whole deals with the Existence (*quia es*) and Perfect Nature (*quia hoc es*) of God. Both are presupposed as revealed and believed: *credimus*. For faith the question of truth is answered on both sides. But for that very reason it now arises for thought. *Veritas* will not be separated from *veritas cogitationis*; nor *credo* from the task: *ut intelligam*. And *intelligere* means: by presupposing other articles of faith, to perceive the necessity of this article of faith and the sheer impossibility of its denial. It is with this perception as it applies to the Existence and Perfect Nature of God that the *Proslogion* is concerned.

Et quidem credimus te esse aliquid quo nihil maius cogitari possit. (I 101, 4f)	But we believe: Thou art 'something beyond which nothing greater can be conceived'.

With this sentence is introduced, as an article of faith, one presupposition of the two proofs that are to be furnished in the *Proslogion*. It has already been fully discussed. The formula that replaces the *tu* spoken in prayer, is the formula for the Name of God as it is manifest to the believer who desires to know it. It conceals no declaration about the Nature of God and still less about God's Existence. The formula simply repeats the injunction inculcated on the believer's thinking by the revelation (*credimus te esse . . .*) not to imagine anything greater than God on pain of the consequence that the conception of a 'God' alongside such a greater than he would immediately cease to be a conception of the true God, that is of the God revealed and believed. For the one who seeks according to the *intellectus fidei,* God is utterly *aliquid quo nihil maius cogitari possit:* unless we recognize this injunction which is inseparable from this object, the object disappears for all knowledge and, if the word *Deus* remains the same, then it must be something different that is meant. The God who is the object of faith, the only One under discussion here, bears this Name. And so in the *Proslogion* Anselm wants to prove the Existence and Perfect Nature of this God.

An ergo non est aliqua talis natura, quia '*dixit insipiens in corde suo non est Deus': ?* (1 101, 5ff)	Is there then no such Nature because 'the fool has said in his heart: there is no God'?

With this question Anselm turns to the problem of the Existence of God and that in the first instance in its universal sense: the problem of the independence of his Existence as against the Existence which he can have in human thinking. Here also *est* means *existit. Aliqua talis natura*: a real thing, an object of this Name. The concept of Existence thus lies in both subject and the predicate of the statement of the question: is the object which, according to what has just been assumed, bears this Name, not really an object at all? This question concerns not faith itself, but thinking within faith, because the assertion 'God is not a real object' is possible and real. The perfect—*dixit insipiens,* which Anselm takes over here from Ps. 13.1 in its Vulgate form—stresses that this assertion is something that has occurred. Because such an objection is lodged the question is therefore a real one for faith's thinking: when the unbeliever explicitly says 'no', then the believer must clearly and explicitly assert 'yes'. That is to say he is called upon to think as necessary what is believed about the inconceivable existence of God. From this objection it would appear to follow that God can be thought of as existing merely in thought, that the assertion of his independent existence may also be understood as hypothesis, fiction, deceit or error. There exists no necessity in fact to understand the sentence: *est aliqua talis natura*—as a positive statement instead of as a question. On those, however, who so understand it, falls the task of balancing the missing factual, outward necessity of this understanding with a demonstration of its objective, inner necessity and so showing this objection which is actually possible to be in fact mistaken and thus rejecting it. But where does this objection come from? By its very origin is it not compromised and liable to rejection without discussion? Is it of such weight that the believer should acknowledge himself as bound to answer it? In actual fact, just as Anselm understands the thesis *Deus est* as not just a logical possibility but qualified as the thesis of faith, so also at once the antithesis, *Deus non est*, is not just a logical possibility corresponding to the previous one, but is qualified or disqualified, as the antithesis of lack of faith. It is the fool who says, 'there is no God'. Anselm read the Psalm only in the Vulgate. Nevertheless, his *insipiens* is scarcely different from the *nabal* of the original text. All that we know about him— what he lacks is not intellectual endowment and erudition; he is not stupid but behaves stupidly; he is quite clever but he is following a principle that is from the outset perverse and pernicious, because he does not know the fear of the Lord, because he has fallen away from God[1]—all that holds more or less clearly of Anselm's *insipiens* also. Neither ought we to allow ourselves to be misled by the (ironical) description of him as *stultus et insipiens* at the end of *Prosl. 3*. According to the same chapter the absurdity of his thinking is that it is nothing to him that he exalts himself as creature above the Creator. According to *Prosl. 4* he is not *intelligens id quod Deus est*.[2]

[1] For these phrases I am indebted to the kindness of my colleague, Lic. Dr M. Thilo of Bonn.

[2] I 103, 21.

Therefore, it is not because of narrow-mindedness or lack of education that he can think: *quia Deus non est*. In the end, in view of the intractable purpose of his counter-thesis, all that Anselm can do is leave him alone and let him go on reiterating it till the last day. But there is a further consideration to be taken into account: if it can be assumed that Anselm had before him the quotation from Ps. 13.1 in its context in the Vulgate text,[1] then at the mention of the *insipiens* he was bound to think of Augustine's *massa perditionis* which is usually identified with the whole of humanity—the *massa perditionis* in which God can abandon the individual by not setting him free, so that by means of this very sacrifice which corresponds to his divine righteousness, he may condemn the man in himself, or rather his unredeemed human nature.[2] While the believer thinks differently from the fool he implicitly recognizes his human solidarity with him and the grace of God as the only thing that can break through and annul this solidarity. In view of this break-through from above, obviously his statement and that of the *insipiens* do not simply represent logical contradictions, but are first and foremost symbols of two radically different modes of human existence determined by a fundamentally different attitude of man to God; ultimately they are expressions of two quite different judgments over against God himself. It might be thought that Anselm could and ought to have declined discussion with the fool *a limine*. But he himself must know! The question with which he is confronted by the objection of the *insipiens* as to the objective, inner necessity of the article of faith in God's existence is not new to him: the foolishness of man without God was not the only or even the

---

1 *Dixit insipiens in corde suo: Non est Deus! Corrupti sunt, et abominabiles facti sunt in studiis suis; non est qui faciat bonum, non est usque ad unum. Dominus de coelo prospexit super filios hominum, ut videat, si est intelligens aut requirens Deum. Omnes declinaverunt, simul inutiles facti sunt; non est qui faciat bonum; non est usque ad unum. . . .* It is most remarkable that the point in question is the same passage as Paul cites (Rom. 3.9) as proof of the general, complete defection of the Jews and Greeks.

2 Cf. to this Anselmic doctrine of reprobation: *De casu diab. 18–20:* I 263ff; *De conc. virg. 25:* II 168f; *De concordia Qu. II 2:* II 261.

first thing to confront him with this question, but rather the *fides quaerens intellectum* itself—*unum idemque est quod quaerimus.*[1] Thinking, albeit differently from him, the believer time and time again finds himself in this human solidarity with the *insipiens*, whose objection serves to remind the believer of his own task, and he cannot refuse to make his answer. Even though there may be no agreement between him and the *insipiens* till the end of time, yet the *insipiens* of today might be the believer of tomorrow and even today he must be summoned to have a part in the response of faith.

Sed certe ipse idem insipiens, cum audit hoc ipsum quod dico: 'aliquid quo maius nihil cogitari potest', intelligit quod audit. . . . (I 101, 7f)	But most certainly even this fool recognizes what he hears when he hears what I say: 'something beyond which nothing greater can be conceived'. . . .

It is important to note the form in which the decisive presupposition is introduced that 'God' means *aliquid quo maius nihil cogitari potest—cum audit hoc ipsum quod dico.* Anselm could not have begun less philosophically. He has absolutely no thought whatsoever of reaching an agreement with his opponent in the debate (or with himself in his capacity as a philosopher) over a universal minimum knowledge of God, still less of becoming involved in a movement towards his opponent's basis of argument. He himself defines what is to be meant by 'God' in the discussion: he speaks and the other has to listen.[2] This procedure, which is not entirely self-evident, becomes obvious when he has interpreted the basis of the discussion that he himself laid down, the definition of the Name of God as an article of faith or revelation. This was to be assumed as already made known if the attempt to understand the other article of revelation concerning the Existence of God were to be tackled

---

[1] Cf. p. 66.

[2] Anselm would have had to express himself quite differently had he conceived the *quo maius cogitari nequit* according to the ideas of the Scholastics of the thirteenth century (cf. p. 77, n. 1, above) as part of the general stock of thought and language.

sensibly.[1] And so this opening of the discussion is itself an implicit challenge to the *insipiens* to believe: this Name might be new to him, it could have the power as *verbum praedicantium Christum* to bring him to the point where he would no longer think as *insipiens* and therefore surely with a different result. But this qualified sense of *dico* and the possibility of an equally qualified *audit* remain latent. All that *dico* means explicitly is— I utter this formula; and *audit*—he hears it in the physical sense; and (this is how Anselm explains himself later), he understands it grammatically and logically.[2] If this *audit* is assumed then, Anselm goes on, we may assert: *intelligit quod audit*. This means: he, the fool who in his heart denies the Existence of God, on hearing this formula cannot avoid thinking it over and considering it to himself in its literal meaning (whatever he may make of it)—God is the One who manifests himself in the command not to imagine a greater than he. The later formulation of this conclusion shows that Anselm kept in mind and reckoned with the fact that the *insipiens* is able to repeat the wording of this formula and, on the presupposition of what he understands by its literal meaning, can deny the existence of the God thus described: at this he charges the *insipiens* with being unable to bring about this negation without at the same time at least conceiving the Name of God and so assuming responsibility for the meaning of what he denies.[3]

---

[1] Briefly at the beginning of the reply to Gaunilo possible objection to this basis of discussion is considered—it was not expressly raised by Gaunilo. But it is immediately dismissed with an appeal to faith—*Si 'quo maius cogitari non potest' non intelligitur vel cogitatur . . . profecto Deus . . . non est quo maius cogitari non possit . . . Quod quam falsum sit, fide . . . tua pro firmissimo utor argumento* (C. Gaun. *1:* I 130, 12ff).

[2] *Utique qui non intelligit, si nota lingua dicitur, aut nullum aut nimis obrutum habet intellectum* (C. Gaun. *2:* I 132, 11ff).

[3] *Etsi quisquam est tam insipiens, ut dicat non esse aliquid quo maius non possit cogitari, non tamen ita erit impudens, ut dicat se non posse intelligere aut cogitare quid dicat. Aut si quis talis invenitur, non modo sermo eius est respuendus, sed et ipse conspuendus. Quisquis igitur negat aliquid esse quo maius nequeat cogitari: utique intelligit et cogitat negationem quam facit. Quam negationem intelligere aut cogitare non potest sine partibus eius. Pars autem eius est 'quo maius cogitari non potest'. Quicumque igitur hoc negat, intelligit et cogitat 'quo maius cogitari nesquit'* (C. Gaun. *9:* I 138, 11ff). Here also we may note how as a foregone conclusion Anselm takes up his position along with his partner on this very presupposition regarding the description of God.

Thus: the suggested Name of God is not some incomprehensible utterance but one that can be understood. The injunction which it brings to expression—whether it be obeyed or not— is clear in itself. Whoever agrees (Anselm does not bother much about this agreement, Anselm dictates) always to interpret in future the word *Deus* by the formula *quo maius cogitari nequit*, cannot subsequently come forward with the complaint that for him the literal meaning of 'God' is a sound that has no meaning.

. . . et quod intelligit, in intellectu eius est, etiam si non intelligat illud esse.	. . . and what he knows, exists in his knowledge, even when he does not
(1 101, 8f)	know that it exists.

Esse in intellectu appears later on in our chapter clearly distinguished from *esse in re* and in the discussion with Gaunilo seems to mean the same as *esse in cogitatione*.[1] The expression therefore means: to exist in knowledge, in thinking, in thought: an object that exists as something that is thought; to be something that is thought of as existing. Anselm makes a fourth division that now points in an altogether new direction (1. *dicere*, 2. *audire*, 3. *intelligere*, 4. *in intellectu esse*). He does not immediately pursue the point that the hearer of this formula is now able to reflect upon it, but rather claims that even for the *insipiens* this formula does describe something or someone. The formula is spoken to him as the formula of a name, as a description of the word *Deus*, which is itself a verbal symbol for the One round whom the discussion centres—the Almighty. In conceiving this formula he therefore also conceives this problematical Almighty; he conceives what is designated *quo maius cogitari nequit* as existing, as an object. Or put the other way round: this problematical Almighty is now something he conceives as an object and as existing.[2] This is even the case

---

[1] *C. Gaun. 1*: 1 130, 13.

[2] Cf. with this A. Koyré's description: *Avoir quelque chose dans l'intelligence n'est que la manière la plus générale de dire que cette même chose est l'objet d'un acte intellectuel. On pourrait peut-être dire que dans le cas, où l'on se représente l'objet comme existent, on l'a dans l'intelligence avec son existence. L'être que l'on a dans l'intelligence n'est pas une*

'when he does now know that it exists', that is, not only when he cannot conceive the existence of this problematical Almighty as more than a concept, but when as *insipiens* he actually denies it. This passage is clarified in various respects by the passages in the discussion with Gaunilo that specially deal with it.

1. Gaunilo interpreted Anselm correctly when he formulated his opinion as follows: on the basis simply of knowing this formula, in that knowledge, God is present.[1]

2. Gaunilo interpreted Anselm no less correctly when—going beyond the literal meaning of this passage but in accordance with Anselm's own argument subsequently sharpened and just quoted[2]—he expounded Anselm's view to the effect that even the man who denies or doubts the existence of God 'has' God existing *in intellectu*.[3]

3. Anselm later interpreted his statement by saying that all he wanted to establish was that there is a knowledge at least on the part of certain men in which God has existence.[4] This conclusion he bases on the somewhat confusing question which he obviously intends ironically: whether something that is proved to have true and necessary existence can exist in no man's knowledge?[5] Naturally what is assumed here can only be what the Existence Proof attempts to do and not what it succeeds in doing: what could for certain men be the object of a proof of its (true) existence must have prior (problematical) existence in their knowledge. There are such men, as *figura*

---

copie, une image, une représentation ou un symbole de l'être réel. C'est cet être lui-même. In intellectu esse ne veut dire qu'être l'objet d'une intention intellectuelle, avoir une existence intentionelle (L'idée de Dieu, etc., pp. 208f).

[1] *Quod hoc iam esse dicitur in intellectu meo, non ob aliud, nisi quia id, quod dicitur, intelligo . . .* (Pro insip. 2: I 125, 14f). Cf. Anselm's own recapitulation: *dixi quia si intelligitur, est in intellectu* (C. Gaun. 2: I 132, 14).

[2] *Cf.* p. 107, n. 3.

[3] *. . . quod ipse negans vel ambigens de illa (sc. natura) iam habeat eam in intellectu, cum audiens illam dici, id quod dicitur, intelligit* (Pro insip. 1: I 125, 4ff).

[4] *. . . 'quo maius cogitari nequit', si est in ullo intellectu. . . .* (C. Gaun. 2: I 132, 30f).

[5] *An est in nullo intellectu, quod necessario in rei veritate esse monstratum est?* (ibid. I 132, 14f).

shows. *Ergo: Deus est in ullo intellectu.* And even on this understanding the statement is sufficient for Anselm's purpose.

4. Following immediately from this question (the whole context is somewhat elastic) Anselm presumes that his opponent will concede the *esse Dei in intellectu* in some sense but throw doubt on the *intelligere* of this *esse.*[1] Anselm does not at first embark on the question of this *intelligere* but demonstrates once more the logical necessity of the step from *intelligere (sc. quod audit)* to *see in intellectu.*[2] He assumes the following to be known and agreed. (1) That in the actual event of thinking (*cogitatio*), by virtue of the act of thought (*cogitare*), there takes place a representation of what is thought (*quod cogitatur*)—(something is thought)—so that it can be said of what is thought in this event and by virtue of this act: it exists in and with this event (*est in cogitatione*). (2) That the *intellectus* is a special form of the *cogitatio* and the *intelligere* is a special form of the *cogitare*, so that this rule is to be applied to them too. From these premises it follows that where something becomes known, as for example the object described as *quo maius cogitari nequit*, a representation of this object takes place by virtue of the act of knowing (*intelligere*) and within the event of knowledge (*intellectus*), so that we may say of it: it exists in and with this event (*est in intellectu.*[3] Just here we have to bear in mind the reservation that was made in the *Proslogion* passage itself: *etiam si non intelligat illud esse.* The question is still by no means settled whether or not this event is due to a voluntary or involuntary deception (in respect of the extramental existence of the object represented). All that it says and shows is that in this event a representation of this object as such invariably takes place and therefore its intramental existence can be asserted.

5. Against the conclusion reached in our text Gaunilo raised

---

[1] *Sed dices quia etsi est in intellectu, non tamen consequitur quia intelligitur (ibid.:* I 132, 15f).

[2] *Vide, quia consequitur esse in intellectu ex eo quia intelligitur (ibid.:* I 132, 16f).

[3] *Sicut enim quod cogitatur, cogitatione cogitatur, et quod cogitatione cogitatur, sicut cogitatur, sic est in cogitatione: ita quod intelligitur intellectu intelligitur, et quod intellectu intelligitur, sicut intelligitur, ita est in intellectu. Quid hoc planius? (ibid.:* I 132, 17ff).

two objections. They are not directed against its validity, which Gaunilo tacitly seems rather to acknowledge, but against the significance which Anselm is prepared to attach to it. The first objection is: on Anselm's view, objects whether they genuinely exist or not can equally well have existence ascribed to them.[1] Anselm's reply to this could simply be that in sustaining such an argument Gaunilo is wasting his breath. The statement to be proved, *Deus est (in intellectu et) in re*, is first to be established in the general and ambiguous and not very clear form—*Deus est in intellectu*. What had first to be shown was whether in this form it was to have limited (*in solo intellectu*) or extended (*in intellectu et in re*) interpretation, whether, that is, the *dubium* is in fact *falsum* or *verum*. How could Gaunilo expect this result to be already obvious in the presupposition?[2] Naturally in knowledge there do exist things that exist only in knowledge and (accepting the contention that in true objectivity *vera* would have to exist in another way also, namely, *in re*) to that extent they are *falsa*.[3] And naturally knowledge of the real existence of the things specified by Anselm's formula is not a general but a special knowledge: what has to be determined is whether it specifies a 'true' or 'false' object. But how far does this represent an objection against the presupposition: *Deus est in intellectu audientis et intelligentis 'quo maius cogitari nequit'?*[4] In fact we shall have to say that this objection was already met by the

---

[1] *Nonne et quaecumque falsa ac nullo prorsus modo in seipsis existentia in intellectu habere similiter dici possem, cum ea, dicente aliquo, quaecumque ille diceret, ego intelligerem?* Gaunilo holds that this *esse in intellectu* is consummated *eo modo, quo etiam falsa quaeque vel dubia haberi possit in cogitatione . . . in quo (sc. in intellectu meo, cum auditum intelligo) similiter esse posse quaecumque alia incerta vel etiam falsa ab aliquo, cuius verba intelligerem dicta (Pro insip. 2: 1 125, 15ff; 126, 11f).*

[2] *Miror quid hic sensisti contra me dubium probare volentem, cui primum hoc sat erat, ut quolibet modo illud intelligi et esse in intellectu ostenderem, quatenus consequenter consideraretur, utrum esset in solo intellectu, velut falsa, an et in re, ut vera (C. Gaun. 6: 1 136, 4ff).*

[3] *Nam si falsa et dubia hoc modo intelliguntur et sunt in intellectu, quia cum dicuntur, audiens intelligit quid dicens significet, nihil prohibet quod dixi intelligi et esse in intellectu (ibid.: 1 136, 8ff).*

[4] *Quodsi et falsa aliquo modo intelliguntur, et non omnis sed cuiusdam intellectus est haec definitio: non debui reprehendi quia dixi 'quo maius cogitari non possit' intelligi et in intellectu esse, etiam antequam certum esset re ipsa illud existere (ibid.: 1 136, 17ff).*

reservation which Anselm himself made in our *Proslogion* passage.

6. Gaunilo's second and cleverer objection is this: granted that the object designated *quo maius cogitari nequit*, just by this name being spoken and heard, exists within the knowledge of the hearer, is an object—yet this happens in such a manner as cannot be conceived.[1] It has, so to speak, only an existence intended by thought, namely the existence which thinking endeavours (in vain) to ascribe to an object which is described to it as existing but which as existing is totally unknown to it.[2] Gaunilo makes these statements on the following basis: we know the object designated *quo maius cogitari nequit* as little as we know that designated *Deus* as an object known to us on the grounds of a definite perception or something analogous to such a definite perception.[3] Indeed this object is unknown to us, either directly or indirectly, which is the same as Anselm's description of it as unique (and therefore not to be inferred even indirectly).[4] A man falsely described to us as existing, we could at least conceive of as existing, because we know at least in general what is meant by human existence. But in no sense can we thus conceive of the existence of God; we can only do so on the basis of the word that we hear about it. But, Gaunilo adds somewhat uncertainly, on the mere basis of a word we could 'hardly ever, indeed never' imagine something to be true[5]—by which he means: understand by the thing to be

---

[1] *Si 'esse' dicendum est in intellectu, quod secundum veritatem cuiusquam rei nequit saltem cogitari, et hoc in meo sic 'esse' non denego (Pro insip. 5: I 127, 28f).*

[2] *Ego enim nondum dico, immo etiam nego vel dubito, ulla re vera esse maius illud, nec aliud ei 'esse' concedo quam illud, si dicendum est 'esse', cum secundum vocem tantum auditam rem prorsus ignotam sibi conatur animus effingere (ibid.: I 128, 4ff).*

[3] *Illud omnibus quae cogitari possint maius . . . tam ego secundum rem vel ex specie mihi vel ex genere notam, cogitare auditum vel in intellectu habere non possum, quam nec ipsum Deum (ibid. 4: I 126, 30–127, 2).*

[4] *Neque enim aut rem ipsam novi aut ex alia possum conicere simili, quandoquidem et tu talem asseris illam, ut esse non possit simile quicquam (ibid.: I 127, 3f).* Gaunilo may be thinking here of the whole contents of *Prosl. 5–26.*

[5] *Nec sici gitur ut haberem falsum istud* (the existence of this man who does not exist) *in cogitatione vel in intellectu, habere possum illud, cum audio dici 'Deus' aut 'aliquid omnibus maius' cum, quando illud secundum rem veram mihique notam cogitare possem, istud omnino nequeam nisi tantum secundum vocem, secundum quam solam aut vix aut numquam potest ullum cogitari verum (ibid.: I 127, 11ff).*

conceived as existing not only the sound of the letters and syllables (which naturally 'exist') of the word that is heard but also the thing that the word signifies,[1] and actually attribute the thought of God's existence (and therefore his existence in thought) to the thinking of someone who has no knowledge of God's existence from any other source,[2] but only this word he has heard! For an understanding of Anselm's reaction to this objection there are three elements in his reply which should be noted:

(a) Right at the beginning of this essay in the passage that we have already quoted more than once, Anselm declares it impossible for a Christian like Gaunilo to act as if he knew nothing at all about what the formula *quo maius cogitari nequit* describes. Perhaps the *insipiens* does know nothing (for he may remain *insipiens* even after the Name of God is proclaimed to him) but at least Gaunilo, as spokesman for the *insipiens*, shares Anselm's knowledge of the *esse Dei in intellectu*. As a Christian he has part in this event of the *intellectus*, he is subject of an action of the *intelligere* and is therefore charged with it and called as a witness that in this event as such the *esse Dei* is reality.[3] At least *in ullo intellectu*[4] God is not just a vain intention but an object that is known.

(b) Recapitulating what was said earlier in connection with this object:[5] knowledge of the inconceivability of God cannot be played off against knowledge of his (intramental) existence because as knowledge of God and therefore knowledge of faith

---

[1] *Siquidem cum ita cogitatur, non tam vox ipsa quae res est utique vera, hoc est litterarum sonus vel syllabarum, quam vocis auditae significatio cogitetur (ibid.:* 1 127, 15ff).

[2] *Ita ut (sc. cogitatur) . . . ab eo qui illud non novit et solummodo cogitat secundum animi motum illius auditu vocis effectum significationemque perceptae vocis conantem effingere sibi. Quod mirum est, si umquam rei veritate potuerit. Ita ergo, nec prorsus aliter, adhuc in intellectu meo constat illud haberi, cum audio intelligoque dicentem esse aliquid maius omnibus quae valeant cogitari (ibid.:* 1 127, 17ff).

[3] *Ego vero dico: si 'quo maius cogitari non potest' non intelligitur vel cogitatur nec est in intellectu vel cogitatione: profecto Deus . . . non est in intellectu vel cogitatione. Quod quam falsum sit . . . conscientia tua pro firmissimo utor argumento. Ergo 'quo maius cogitari non potest' vere intelligitur et cogitatur et est in intellectu et cogitatione (C. Gaun. 1:* 1 130, 12ff).

[4] Cf. p. 109, n. 4.   [5] Cf. pp. 79ff.

it rather presupposes this latter. It excludes far more radically than Gaunilo appears to assume an intuitive knowledge on our part of God's Existence. If, by this objection, Gaunilo really was thinking of the inconceivability of God then he must have known that there was absolutely no question whatsoever of a knowledge of God's existence *secundum veritatem cuiusquam rei*[1] (that is, for example, corresponding to the knowledge we can have of a man's existence) and that consequently the impossibility of it should not have been introduced as an argument against knowledge of his existence. But combined with this fatal flaw in his technical knowledge is the fact that for him *quo maius cogitari nequit* is just one *percepta vox* amongst many others and is not a dynamic word of revelation ; it is not the Name of God that is revealed and believed. His failure to understand God's inconceivability now shows itself in that he does not see that as this is ever confirmed by definite qualified *voces* which for that very reason are more than just the noise of letters and syllables, so it is also cancelled. As a Christian (as was shown under (*a*))—he could not treat these *voces* and *in concreto* the *vox 'quo maius cogitari nequit'* as he was doing. By so doing he avoids the necessity, or rather, denies himself the possibility, of facing this: to hear and understand this Name involves an *aliquatenus intelligere* of existence in so far as the person hearing and understanding is by no means confronted by a mere word (such as the word '*Deus*') but by a prohibition which certainly does not contain or express anything about the existence of God but which nonetheless by setting a definite limit on concepts of God, describes existence *in intellectu.* From this point we can at least catch a glimpse (as a problem) of the contents of the statement of faith in question concerning the existence of God awareness of which came to us from elsewhere, so that we cannot hear it without at the same time becoming aware of the existence of this same God who makes the prohibition (which is nothing like the existence of a mere

[1] Cf. p. 112, n. 1.

114

X). Just as something conceivable is said by the statement of God's inconceivability and therefore God is described in a definite way without his being turned into a quantity that can be conceived, so the Name of God describes him whose name it is—*aliquatenus*, in the noetic sphere, in the form of a mere definition; but none the less it does describe him.[1] The hesitant 'hardly ever, or indeed never'[2] in Gaunilo's denial of the intellectual power of all *voces* would appear to indicate that at this point our opponent himself is not quite sure of his case. How indeed could he be?

(*c*) The argument so far adduced against the objection (that God's existence for our knowledge on the basis of hearing his Name is simply the existence of something utterly unknown to us) left out of account, with Gaunilo, the fact that along with God's Name and his existence which is being proved here, God's Nature is also revealed. If this is taken into account, as is reasonable, then the objection becomes absolutely impossible. It should be noted that there is no question whatsoever of Anselm's appeal to this point of view being used to prove the proposition that God exists from the statement of his Nature.[3] All that is involved is: whoever hears the Name of God can— whether he does so is a different question, but he can— 'thereby conceive something' because, if he really hears, he cannot possibly lack a revelation of the Nature of God and that is the point here. And to the extent to which he is able to do that he can hardly dispute the existence of God in his consciousness on the ground that for him the Name of God is an empty concept. Anselm came to mention this in two passages of his essay against Gaunilo and from two different standpoints.

---

[1] *Sicut enim nil prohibet dici 'ineffabile', licet illud dici non possit quod 'ineffabile' dicitur: et quemadmodum cogitari potest 'non cogitabile', quamvis illud cogitari non possit cui convenit 'non cogitabile' dici: ita cum dicitur 'quo nil maius valet cogitari', procul dubio quod auditur cogitari et intelligi potest, etiam si res illa cogitari non valeat aut intelligi, qua maius cogitari nequit* (*C. Gaun. 9:* I 138, 6ff).

[2] Cf. p. 112, n. 5.

[3] Everything that has to be said here, except the question of existence which has to be settled on other grounds, holds good—*etiam si non credat in re esse quod cogitat . . . sive sit in re aliquid huiusmodi sive non sit* (*C. Gaun. 8:* I 137, 19 and 23f).

In the first place, summarizing what Gaunilo could read in *Prosl. 13* and *18-22*, he showed how on the basis of the formula *quo maius cogitari nequit* it is also possible to comprehend the indivisible eternity and omnipresence of God: only the non-eternal and non-omnipresent, therefore only the finite can be conceived as non-existing. God—assuming that he exists—cannot be conceived as non-existing. Something conceivable as non-existing, even were it to exist, would not be God, would not be *quo maius cogitari nequit*. Thus God must be the One who is indivisibly eternal and omnipresent. Assuming once more that God's Nature is utterly beyond conceiving, which these concepts do not deny but rather assert, assuming that total veiling wherein God becomes conceivable to us as eternal and omnipresent in his very unveiling—God's eternity and omnipresence being revealed to us, their necessity becoming intelligible on the basis of the formula *quo maius cogitari nequit*—assuming this, knowledge of what is described as *quo maius cogitari nequit* does occur even although it be noetically limited and touches the actual object only from the outside; consequently it has existence in our knowledge as a subject[1] known to us at all times and in all places. In this connection Anselm has to remind us of a second point. The second half of Gaunilo's statement: *neque enim aut rem ipsam novi aut ex alia possum conicere simili*[2]—is not valid in this absolute form. The man who is outside the Church, the man who is without revelation and faith, knows nothing in actual practice about

---

[1] *Quare quidquid alicubi aut aliquando totum non est, etiam si est, potest cogitari non esse. At 'quo maius nequit cogitari': si est(!), non potest cogitari non esse; alioquin si est, non est quo maius cogitari non possit, quod non convenit. Nullatenus ergo alicubi aut aliquando totum non est, sed semper et ubique totum est. Putasne aliquatenus posse cogitari vel intelligi aut esse in cogitatione vel intellectu, de quo haec intelliguntur? . . . Certe vel hactenus intelligitur et est in intellectu 'quo maius cogitari nequit', ut haec de eo intelligantur (C. Gaun. 1:* I 131, 31–132, 9). The chapter *C. Gaun. 1* is not well arranged, because Anselm first of all reproduces Gaunilo's objections thus (I 130, 20ff): *Putas* [1] *ex eo quia intelligitur aliquid quo maius cogitari nequit, non consequi illud esse in intellectu,* [2] *nec si est in intellectu, ideo esse in re*—but, then in reply (I 131, 1ff) he proceeds with [1] three new facets of the Proof in the form of *Prosl. 3* and [2] the note on the *esse in intellectu* (I 131, 18–132, 9).

[2] *Pro insip. 4:* I 127, 2.

him who bears the Name *quo maius cogitari nequit,* whom the Church confesses as the *summum bonum nullo alio indigens et quo omnia indigent.*[1] Outside the Church there is in practice no *conicere Deum.* There is nothing in the world which is *simile* to human reason as such and *per se,* which is necessary to it and which quite independently of anything outside of itself is also a medium for knowledge of God. That there should be such media requires the existence of the Church, revelation and faith. In so far as man is viewed in himself and apart from the Church, God is in fact an object which he neither knows directly nor indirectly. But that does not mean that within his world man cannot know God or that the things of this world cannot become for him *similia* of God. As we saw earlier[2] even the Church's knowledge and faith's knowledge is knowledge *per similitudinem.* Here, within the Church, there takes place a *conicere,* an inference from experience of the world as to the nature of God just as truly as this does not take place outside the Church. Here, 'ascending' (*conscendendo*) beyond relative, finite, material things—conscious of the inadequacy of the insights and statements that can be achieved—this *summum bonum* actually becomes accessible. The revelation is the revelation of God in his world, in the world which is so constituted that God's Nature can be manifest therein *in speculo, per similitudinem, per analogiam* (as far as God wills to reveal himself and has in fact revealed himself), even if in fact it is manifest to no one. With its knowledge of God the Church actualizes a possibility open to mankind[3] but of which mankind as such cannot avail itself in practice because of the Fall—yet, for that very reason, a possibility whose reality must be insisted upon, and which within the Church can be realized. The answer to the *insipiens* who denies the existence of God because he is unable to conceive anything by the word 'God', should

---

[1] *Prosl. Prologue:* I 93, 8.   [2] Cf. pp. 29f.

[3] Which obviously does not reside in its created nature as such but in the fact of its being created in the image of God in creaturely dependence on the Son who from all eternity knows the Father.

therefore be that as a man he would be well able to do so were
he not also *homo insipiens*. The Catholic however ought to consider Rom. 1.20 and should not protect the *insipiens* in this
respect. The attempt to conceive of something by the word
'God' and therefore of the *esse Dei in intellectu* must not break
down because God is a hidden God. As such he is also the God
who is manifest, who even reveals himself in the real world of
the *insipiens*. There is a *conicere Deum*. Where and when it
actually happens is of course another question.[1]

Aliud enim est rem esse in intellectu, aliud intelligere rem esse. Nam cum pictor praecogitat quae facturus est, habet quidem in intellectu, sed nondum intelligit esse quod nondum fecit. Cum vero iam pinxit, et habet in intellectu et intelligit esse quod iam fecit. (I 101, 9ff)	The existence of an object in knowledge is one thing, knowledge of its existence is another. For when an artist thinks out in advance what he is going to create, then he certainly has it in his mind but he knows that what he has not yet created does not yet exist. But his painting once finished, then he both has it in his mind and he knows that what he has now created does exist.

What we have before us in this exposition is the very unambiguous development of Anselm's (general) concept of
knowledge of existence. It connects with the condition attached
to the previous quotation that what a man knows has existence
in his knowledge even if he does not know of its existence. This
paradox obviously calls for comment. If the first statement is
true like the one following it with the condition attached, then
the concept *intelligere*, as well as the concept *esse* (*existere*),
must have been used in both cases in different senses. This is
precisely the opinion that Anselm at once goes on to express.
We may conceive a thing as existing without knowing whether

---

[1] *Quoniam namque omne minus bonum in tantum est simile maiori bono inquantum est bonum: patet cuilibet rationabili menti, quia de bonis minoribus ad maiora conscendendo ex iis quibus aliquid maius cogitari potest, multum possumus conicere illud quo nihil potest maius cogitari . . . Sic itaque facile refelli potest insipiens qui sacram auctoritatem non recipit, si negat 'quo maius cogitari non valet' ex aliis rebus conici posse. At si quis catholicus hoc neget, meminerit quia 'invisibilia Dei a creatura mundi per ea quae facta sunt intellecta conspiciuntur, sempiterna quoque eius virtus et divinitas'* (C. Gaun. 8: I 137, 14–138, 3).

it exists and even although it has existence only in our knowledge. Its existence in knowledge and awareness of its existence in knowledge are to be distinguished; moreover, we would obviously have to distinguish between its existence apart from the limitation of knowledge, its real existence that is not merely intended or imagined, and the knowledge of such existence—knowledge that strikes out beyond the limits of knowledge and knows real existence. Thus far Anselm has shown that God has existence in this first sense and may be known as existing where his Name is proclaimed, heard and understood. But *aliud—aliud*. He hastens to explain that not till then is the question of existence raised, not till then is the object in dispute described. What is dealt with in the Proof of the Existence of God is existence and knowledge of existence in the second sense. It was absolutely essential to make sure of the existence of God in the first sense and we shall be reminded later that this has been done. But Anselm made sure first of all of the problem, the *dubium*; in no sense does this bring the problem nearer any kind of solution. It must still first be shown, by asserting the second sense of these concepts, whether the *dubium* was true or false. The *intelligere rem esse*, the proof of which has still to come, also determines the truth of the *esse rei in intellectu*. This starting-point, the point immediately before the beginning of the Proof proper (in its general form), is illustrated by the picture of the relation between an artist's idea and his work. The *tertium comparationis* consists in this (and in this alone): there is an intramental existence of objects as well as one that is both intramental and extramental; thus there is also a corresponding double knowledge of existence. The second is the true, real knowledge of existence to which the first is related as an artistic conception that may bear fruit or may be for ever barren is related to the work of art that may issue from it as its fulfilment, vindication and justification. At any rate, the distinction that has to be made here is overshadowed by this preliminary distinction. And it is precisely when the theory of existence has to follow the reality of existence, when thought of the existence of the object has to follow its existence, that the theory first comes up against this preliminary distinction, the ambiguous *esse rei in intellectu*, and has the right and the duty to assume that this previous distinction does from time to time occur. In two points Gaunilo warns us how not to understand Anselm's artist analogy.

1. Gaunilo complained that on this analogy temporal precedence would necessarily be implied for the *habere rem in intellectu* over the *intelligere rem esse*, whereas on the presuppositions of the *intelligere rem esse* the two must take place simultaneously.[1] This objection is so fantastic that Anselm was quite right hardly to touch on it in his reply.[2] There was absolutely no question at all in the analogy of contrasting precedence in time. Anselm explicitly said in our *Proslogion* passage that on the presuppositions of the *intelligere rem esse* it and the *habere rem in intellectu* happen at one and the same time: *cum vero iam pinxit, et habet in intellectu et intelligit esse*. The fact that Gaunilo questioned the possibility of a neutral *habere rem in intellectu* prior to the *intelligere rem esse*, only goes to show how little he understood the course of Anselm's proof which proceeded so carefully from premiss to conclusion.

2. Gaunilo devoted a whole chapter of his reply,[3] the most enigmatic of all we may say, to proving that Augustine had said[4] that when a carpenter (*faber*) constructs a chest then first of all the artistic sense of the carpenter ponders the creation (*in arte*) of this chest (*arca*) and *arca quae fit in opere non est vita, arca quae est in arte vita est, quia vivit anima artificis*. Debasing Augustine, Gaunilo makes of this: *illa pictura antquam fiat, in ipsa pictoris arte habetur et tale quippiam . . . nihil ese aliud quam pars quaedam intelligentiae ipsius . . . quam scientia vel intelligentia animae ipsius*. However, with the truth of the *quo maius cogitari nequit*—

---

[1] *Non hic erit iam aliud idemque tempore praecedens, habere rem in intellectu, et aliud idque tempore sequens, intelligere rem esse; ut fit de pictura quae prius est in animo pictoris, deinde in opere (Pro insip. 2: I 126, 1ff).*

[2] *C. Gaun. 6: I 136, 19ff.*   [3] *Pro insip. 3: I 126, 14ff.*   [4] *In Joannem, tract. I, 16.*

assuming that it is true and as such is *in intellectu*—it could on no account be the case that it is identical with the *intellectus, quo capitur*. Anselm's reply to this speech was quite short and somewhat ironical: he had not had this application of the analogy (to the primacy of the idea over the finished work and therefore to the creative rôle of man in respect of the existence of God) in mind at all.[1] What serious design and intention there may have been in this part of Gaunilo's essay is in practice difficult to determine. Why does he devote such attention to this opening statement of Anselm's? Why does he not see that Anselm could just as easily have used a different illustration? Why does he bring in just here the giant spectre of Augustine? Does he suddenly sense in Anselm's *habere rem in intellectu*, to which he had just objected because of its neutrality, something akin to Feuerbachianism—the elevation of man to be creator of God?[2] Or is it not worth while searching any further because what we have here is simply an objection of convenience, of embarrassment? However that may be, it is as little calculated to advance the discussion as the first objection.

Convincitur ergo etiam insipiens esse vel in intellectu aliquid quo nihil maius cogitari potest, quia hoc cum audit, intelligit, et quidquid intelligitur, in intellectu est. (I 101, 13ff)	Thus even the fool can be convinced that 'that than which nothing greater can be conceived' exists in his knowledge. For when he hears it, he knows it; and what is known is in knowledge.

[1] *Quod vero tam studiose probas 'quo maius cogitari nequit' non tale esse qualis nondum facta pictura in intellectu pictoris: sine causa fit. Non enim ad hoc protuli picturam praecogitatam, ut tale illud de quo agebatur vellem asserere, sed tantum ut aliquid esse in intellectu, quod esse non intelligeretur, possem ostendere* (C. Gaun. 8: I 137, 6ff).

[2] W. v. d. Steinen, *Der Heilige Geist des Mitteletaers*, 1926, p. 38, interprets ('at this point I insert a secondary thought') Anselm's artistic analogy as follows: 'the artist has the idea of a picture, but it has no reality; however, if he creates the picture, he thereby also creates the reality . . . in the same way an Almighty can also be conceived who is only a conception. But anyone who is a thinker and not a dreamer cannot rest content with this; even in the wildest thinking there resides the law pervading all nature that demands reality and it will not be content until it has also formed what is already complete as an ideal. God has not only prompted us to rely on him . . . ; not only prompted us to conceive him; he has also prompted us to create him as much in living faith as in living thought . . . also the man who thinks clearly, if only his thought be completely logical, wills God.' Why did this author not allow the Anselm passage quoted in the previous note to keep him from this ingenious 'secondary thought'? And why not by perceiving that he who

This statement closes the circle that began above with *Sed certe ipse idem* . . . and confirms the assertion that was then made and has since been proved. Let us now turn back for a moment: up till now our concern has been to settle the object of inquiry. The protest of the *insipiens*, '*non est Deus*', has served to remind even the believing thinker that the problem of the Existence of God is not self-evident. The Existence of God has to be already proved in this first preliminary sense, it has to be shown that the *insipiens* can certainly say in his heart that 'there is no God' —without that succeeding in altering (even when denied by him) anything in respect of the Existence of God and that in particular in his knowledge. From this conclusion which even the unbeliever cannot avoid, the believer also has to be shown where to begin in order that his faith in God's Existence may be brought to knowledge. What has been said so far has been directed to this conclusion. The starting-point for this exposition was not some available or accessible human conviction about God, but it was his Name proclaimed and believed. This Name can be heard and understood of men. In that case it does describe something or someone to men: the one whose name it is thus exists at least *in intellectu* of man, whether believed or not, whether in his true existence accepted or denied. Here, even though perhaps it may be only here, he has existence. Even if anyone wanted to deny this as being inconeivable to him, yet in face of the fact that even evidence for the true existence of God can be produced, he cannot deny that at least for others this hypothesis could be evident. Be that as it may, the fact that knowledge of this Name occurs introduces the problem of God's existence—no more than that. The objection that in this sense this is to introduce the problem of the existence of any absurdity whatsoever overlooks the fact that a premiss is involved which the proof proper has first of all to vindicate without its value as a premiss being thereby impaired. And

so manifestly intended to write in Anselm's praise, with this interpretation was branding himself as one who had clearly inherited Gaunilo's understanding of Anselm?

against the objection that we are unable to conceive of anything that purports to exist *in intellectu,* it can be said on the
other hand that a Christian is not allowed to raise this objection
and that the Name of God is no mere word but a description
where the thing described is also conceivable as present;
that even apart from this there are ample signposts indicating
the nature of the thing described. Real knowledge of existence
is to be distinguished then from this ambiguous type: its real
concern will be knowledge of the existence of God that is also
extramental and indeed this is to be the subject of the main and
decisive proof itself. What has to be established here is that
the assumption of his intramental existence is possible. This
cannot be denied even in the thought of the *insipiens* that denies
God.

Et certe id quo maius cogitari nequit, non potest esse in solo intellectu. (1 101, 15f)	And certainly 'that than which nothing greater can be conceived' cannot exist only in knowledge.

We have now entered upon the Proof proper (first of the
general existence of God—in the restricted sense in which
things that are different from God also exist). This statement
declares what is now to be proved (in sharp contrast to what
resulted from the premiss)—the impossibility of an existence
of God only within knowledge; that means the necessity of his
objective existence, his actual existence. The hypothesis that
God exists in human knowledge (on the grounds that his Name
is proclaimed, heard and understood) is proved by what has
been already said. This existing in knowledge is a problematical
existing which has first to be examined in respect of its truth.
The universal criterion of the truth of a thing that exists
(applicable to God as to all that exists) is just the opposite of
this limit 'existing in knowledge'. If God exists in truth he
cannot exist merely in knowledge. Truth is not primarily in
knowledge, but only secondarily so. It is first truth in objects:
it is primarily truth in itself. Truth that was only in knowledge
would be a broken reed. The same could be said of a truth

which was true only in knowledge and in objects but was not true in itself. But at least it is in the first place a criterion of truth that it should be truth not only in knowledge but also in objects. The subject of the Proof is only the negative, first part of this statement: in Truth there exists what exists not only in knowledge; that means, what is known as incapable of existing in knowledge alone is known as existing in Truth. When that is known in relation to God, then the existence of God is proved (always in the narrow sense in which the existence of things other than God can also be proved).

Si enim vel in solo intellectu est, potest cogitari esse et in re . . . (1 101, 16f)

If it exists thus only in knowledge it can also be conceived as existing objectively.

Anselm first assumed the possibility, the premiss that the phrase, God exists in knowledge, understood in the restricted sense, is to be taken as definitive: that is, God exists only in knowledge. If this were so, the possibility would none the less remain of removing in thought the parenthesis 'only in knowledge' and of ascribing to this God, contrary to his self-imposed reality, an existence consisting not only in knowledge but also in objectivity. Even the consciousness that this is inconsistent with God's self-imposed reality, which inconsistency is involved in this view, need not deter us. God is called *id quo maius cogitari nequit*. In so far as this Name is the criterion for what may or may not be believed about him, it is not clear to what extent we can refuse to ascribe to him in theory extramental in addition to this intramental existence. It may even be that knowledge of the God who exists *in solo intellectu* instinctively and irresistibly presses to such reality as it assumes here 'only inwardly' with bold and contradictory exaggerations about his existence 'outwardly also'. But even from the point of view of logic there is nothing to prevent such *cogitare*. For it can have no claim on truth in the strict sense but merely regard itself as a reflection of awareness of God in its own consciousness. However figuratively and irresponsibly the *est et in re* may be meant, at least it can always be thought. Perhaps there is no representation at all thus deliberately included in the reservation whose validity was meant only intramentally. By such a representation this reservation would of necessity be openly shattered and a mythologizing *esse in re* would have to be conceived as well, at the borderline of thought. Be that as it may: *potest cogitari et in re.*

. . *quod maius est.*   (I 101, 17) . . . that is greater.

These three words, joined to the twofold possibility just announced, introduce the argument which is crucial for the proof: if (1) God exists only in knowledge and if (2) God can be conceived as existing objectively and not only in knowledge, then it means—a greater is conceivable than he who first assumed to be 'God'. The general rule which is assumed at this point—that a being who exists in knowledge and in addition exists objectively is 'greater' than one who merely exists in knowledge—is no axiom, but an inference from Anselm's doctrines of Truth and Knowledge which are already known to us. If a being exists not only in knowledge but also objectively then for Anselm it must be 'greater' than one existing only in knowledge, because the realm of knowledge forms the third and final level of reality, and the realm of objectivity forms the second, which is directly related to the first level, the realm of Truth itself. Why should something that really exists only in knowledge not be incomparably much 'smaller' than what also exists objectively? Why should this latter not be incomparably much 'greater'? It has the qualitative and not quantitative superiority of the source of all truth (in so far as it is not identical with God) not in itself, but for itself, granted by God, distinct from knowledge. Thus in consequence of this rule, which for Anselm was self-evident, the God who is conceivable and who exists in knowledge and in objectivity is greater and essentially greater than the God who previously was assumed as existing only in knowledge. But just because on Anselm's assumptions the *maius* is essentially greater, a being on a higher level, the conception of this *maius* violates the identity assumed from the start of the *maius* with the *minus* that up till now was presumed to be God, the One who existed *in solo intellectu*. Whoever ascribes both intra- and extramental existence to God is not thinking of the same God as the person for whom God is this *minus*. It is still not settled that this *minus* cannot be identical with God but it should not be overlooked that over against him this *maius* is at the same time an *aliud*, something not identical with him, not a predicate that he can have added himself but a new second subject distinct from him. If we make use in any sense whatever of the possibility of ascribing to the God who is assumed to exist only intramentally, extramental existence as well, then we have to be clear that we have conceived a greater and therefore a different being alongside God. And even if we do not make any use of this possibility, but cannot help recognizing it simply as a possibility, then we cannot deny that theoretically we have placed such a greater and therefore different being alongside the God who claims real existence *in solo intellectu*.

Si ergo id quo maius cogitari non potest, est in solo intellectu: id ipsum quo maius cogitari non potest, est quo maius cogitari potest. Sed certe hoc esse non potest.

(I 101, 17–102, 2)

When, therefore, 'that than which a greater cannot be conceived' exists only in knowledge, then 'that than which a greater cannot be conceived' is such than which a greater can be conceived. But this it clearly cannot be.

We saw that it is possible, going beyond the assumed reality of God's existence *in solo intellectu*, to conceive of God as existing *in intellectu et in re*. But in so doing we do not conceive of the same God but of a being who is different, greater and superior. What is the consequence? The consequence is that it becomes quite impossible to identify this being who exists *in solo intellectu* with God. God is *id quo maius cogitari nequit*. But this being is such, as we have shown, that mentally it is possible to place alongside him a being who is different from him and greater than

him. This first being is thus equated with God in a manner
that is explicitly forbidden by God's Name—conceiving of
God in such a way that something greater than him is conceivable. It is called *quo maius cogitari non potest* and yet it is
a *quo maius cogitari potest*. This contradiction is intolerable:
certe hoc esse non potest. The Name of God cannot apply to this
being.[1] There must be some unfortunate confusion here with
some pseudo-God who is not God. But even the Name of God
that is wrongly attributed to him signifies his unmasking. If
this being who exists only in knowledge is seriously taken for
God, he turns out to be a contradiction in terms, in fact
nothing. The 'God' who only exists in knowledge could only be
a reality on the assumption that he did not make any serious
claim to be God and did not bear the Name of God that for
him is too great. As a fine product of the intellect, as 'God', he
may well survive *in solo intellectu*. But to be identified with
God the least he would need to possess would be the existence
that applies even to the created world: the *esse in intellectu et
in re*.

Existit ergo procul dubio aliquid quo maius cogitari non valet, et in intellectu et in re. (1 102, 2f)	Thus objectively as well as in knowledge there does undoubtedly exist 'something than which nothing greater can be conceived'.

To understand this conclusion we must not simply grasp the
first German translation which comes our way: 'there does
therefore undoubtedly exist something. . . .'[2] Despite the fact

[1] Anselm has offered in *C. Gaun.* 2 (1 132, 14–133, 2) a complete, and in detail
perhaps even fuller, repetition of the train of thought developed here. Worth
noting in confirmation of our interpretation here is the Proof which is given there
of the *certe hoc esse non potest* of our *Proslogion* passage: *utique 'quo maius cogitari potest'
in nullo intellectu est 'quo maius cogitari non possit'* (1 132, 29f).

[2] Thus J. Brinktrine in his translation of the *Proslogion* into German in Ferdinand
Schöningh's *Sammlung philosophischer Lesestoffe*, Paderborn, n.d.)—not a work of any
significance. The translation of H. Bouchitté is quite arbitrary and misleading (*Le
rationalisme chrétien à la fin du XI siècle*, Paris 1842, p. 247): *Il existe donc certainement
un être audessus duquel on ne peut rien imaginer, ni dans la pensée ni dans le fait.* Better,
but not entirely unambiguous because of the absence of quotation marks which
are quite indispensable here, A. Koyré: *Par conséquent il n'y a aucun doute, que
quelque chose dont on ne peut rien concevoir de plus grand existe et dans l'intelligence et dans
la réalité.*

that *existit* is placed first, it follows from the whole content of the chapter that the emphasis of the sentence is not on this *existit*, which in itself is ambiguous, but on what explains it— *et in intellectu et in re*. Not till then does the *existit* become unambiguous in the sense of the desired result. What Anselm regards as having been proved by what has gone before is that the thing described as *aliquid quo maius cogitari non valet* has existence not only in knowledge but also has objective (and to that extent genuine) existence. Now how far has that been proved? In so far as it has been shown that God exists in the knowledge of the hearer when the Name of God is preached, understood and heard. But he cannot exist merely in the knowledge of the hearer because a God who exists merely thus stands in impossible contradiction to his own Name as it is revealed and believed, because, in other words, he would be called God but would not be God. Thus as God he cannot exist in knowledge as the one who merely exists in knowledge.[1] It should be noted that nothing has been proved beyond this negative. The last word of the Proof is *hoc esse non potest*, as also its intention was described only negatively: *Deus non potest esse in solo intellectu.*[2] But the conclusion reaches further: God's existence *et in intellectu et in re* is concluded from the fact that a God who exists *in solo intellectu* has been proved impossible. With what justification? All that is proved is just this negative. The positive statement about the genuine and extramental existence of God (in the general sense of the concept 'existence') does not stem from the proof and is in no sense derived from it but is proved by the proof only in so far as the opposite statement about God's merely intramental existence is shown to be absurd. Where then does this positive statement come from? It was suddenly brought in with the hypothetical *potest cogitari esse*

---

[1] In the parallel *C. Gaun. 2* (I 132, 30ff) the conclusion is in this form which further confirms the paraphrase given in the text: *An ergo non consequitur, 'quo maius cogitari nequit', si est in ullo intellectu, non esse in solo intellectu? Si enim est in solo intellectu, est quo maius cogitari potest; quod non convenit.*

[2] Cf. p. 123.

et in re[1] and it remains now merely because it was proved that the statement to the opposite effect was absurd. If that is a 'proof' then it is the proof of an article of faith which still holds good apart from all proof.[2] The positive statement cannot be traced back as it originates in revelation. And the statement that is opposite to it can only be reduced *ad absurdum* by means of another that likewise comes from revelation, God is *quo maius cogitari nequit*. That, however, can be done. And to that extent the genuine existence of God (in the general sense of the concept 'existence') can be proved and has been proved here.

Nothing is perhaps more significant for the essay *Pro insipiente* than the fact that in the main Gaunilo deals only with the train of thought from *Prosl. 2* that has just been analysed and that in it he sees, like so many of his successors, Anselm's Proof of God.[3] Further—without allowing the doctrine of God in the rest of the *Proslogion* (which he praised) to bring the importance of this matter to his attention, he could pass over the references of *Prosl. 3* which to Anselm were crucial, with a few observations which though not unintelligent in themselves scarcely comprise a seventh part of the total work. In the fact that he regards[4] Anselm's first word as the decisive one, indeed the only one, and Anselm's second word as a mere repetition of the first, and in the ease with which he disposes of this second word, we cannot fail to find proof of our earlier contention that Gaunilo had no interest in the problem that ultimately was the only one of interest to Anselm, the absolutely

[1] Cf. p. 124.

[2] That this is what Anselm means will become evident in *Prosl. 3*, where in the parallel passage, the vital *et hoc es tu Domine, Deus noster* (I 103, 3) appears. Why not here? Obviously because the proof in *Prosl. 2* is only a stage on the way to the proof proper which is not to be worked out till *Prosl. 3*.

[3] *Aux yeux d'Anselme, la preuve est faite*, we read—we can scarcely believe our eyes—at the end of the reference to *Prosl. 2* in the *Dictionnaire de Théol. cath.* vol. I, column 1351.

[4] . . . *cum deinceps asseritur, tale esse maius illud, ut nec sola cogitatione valeat non esse, et hoc rursus non aliunde probatur, quam eo ipso, quod aliter non erit omnibus maius* . . . (*Pro insip. 7: I 129, 1*ff).

unique existence of God. But quite obstinately and in actual
fact very shortsightedly all he demanded was proof that God
exists in the manner of created things. We saw that Anselm
does not deny this but actually proves it in *Prosl. 2. Vere est*
means here: he does not exist only in thought but also exists
over against thought. Why should this sign of true existence
not belong as much to him as to every object of his creation?
But obviously belong to him as God in a totally different way.
That is what the *Proslogion* has still not made clear. By the mere
fact that God exists in just the same way as any other object, the
problem of his existence is still not answered as far as Anselm is
concerned (unlike Gaunilo). God is 'outside', God stands over
against the thinking in the unique manner in which the
Creator stands over against the thinking of the creation. That
is the characteristic force of the article of faith on the Existence
of God. That is what is to be proved in *Prosl. 3.* If Gaunilo had
no interest in this background and aim of Anselm's inquiry how
then was he to understand *Prosl. 2* on its own? We already know
the objections which he had to bring against the introduction to
the Proof of *Prosl. 2* (against the *esse Dei in intellectu* and
against the artist analogy). These elements of his polemic art
apart, the only other proper reference to the point at issue is
in what is expressed most forcibly in the famous island analogy
in the sixth chapter of his work. We have already referred to
this in detail[1] and we can only repeat: Gaunilo refuses to be
satisfied, as we saw, with the mere expression *quo maius cogitari
nequit* and with a proof that is based on hearing and understanding this expression. Thus he is not disputing the correct-
ness of the conclusions that Anselm draws—that alongside the
God who merely exists *in intellectu* something conceivable as existing *in intellectu et in re* would be 'greater' and that therefore an
intolerable contradiction obtains between the Name of God
that is the hypothesis and his existence *in solo intellectu*. What he
is objecting to is the givenness, which Anselm describes, of the

---

[1] Cf. pp. 81 and 95f.

presupposition of these conclusions and therefore also to the result that is reached by means of these conclusions. Who or what this expression describes is completly unknown to us; it would have to be revealed to us somehow, but certainly not just by this expression, in order to witness to its own existence in this its known reality as opposed to something merely existing *in intellectu.*[1] Whereas Anselm's *quo maius cogitari nequit* charms him, Gaunilo likes the description of an incomparably rich and lovely island in the sea, belonging to no one and uninhabited, which *ex difficultate vel potius impossibilitate inveniendi quod non est* is called the 'lost' island. This description he could well understand though quite unable thereby to have it proved that because of its known excellence this island is bound also to exist.[2] We saw already that all this is sheer misunderstanding. Anselm's hypothesis is certainly an expression, but not as Gaunilo thinks empty words, but the Word of God—not as Gaunilo thinks, an expression given and to be understood in isolation, but a Word of God within the context of his revelation, to which also belongs the revelation of his existence. It declares the Name of God from which Name we certainly cannot derive his existence, as Gaunilo interpolates, but from which the impossibility of his non-existence (on the assumption of his revealed, unique existence as Creator—which Gaunilo ignores) is perceived and which makes it possible to recognize in thought the Existence of God that is believed. This result does not satisfy Gaunilo because he himself is obviously in search of a proof of God from some sort of experience, a proof which would have nothing to do with Anselm's *intellectus fidei* and which would be excluded by Anselm's very concept of God.[3]

[1] *Prius enim certum mihi necesse est fiat re vera esse alicubi maius ipsum, et tum demum ex eo quod maius est omnibus, in seipso quoque subsistere non erit ambiguum (Pro insip. 5: 1 128, 11ff).*

[2] *Si, inquam, per haec ille mihi velit astruere de insula illa, quod vere sit, ambigendum ultra non esse: aut iocari illum credam, aut nescio quem stultiorem debeam reputare, utrum me, si ei concedam, an illum, si se putet aliqua certitudine insulae illius essentiam astruxisse (Pro insip. 6: 1 128, 26ff).*

[3] *Eo modo summe sensibilis es, quo summe omnia cognoscis, non quo animal corporeo sensu cognoscit (Prosl. 6: 1 105, 5f).*

In this way then Gaunilo comments on *Prosl.* 2, and in doing so shows he is at cross purposes with Anselm.

2. THE SPECIAL EXISTENCE OF GOD (*Prosl. 3*)

Quod non possit cogitari non esse.	That he could not be conceived as
(1 102, 5)	not existing.

This heading denotes the second, more specific meaning of *vere sit*: God exists in such a way (true only of him) that it is impossible for him to be conceived as not existing.

Quod utique sic vere est, ut nec cogitari	Which so truly exists that it cannot
possit non esse.	even be conceived as not existing.
(1 102, 6)	

We have now to take a look at a second, narrower definition of the general existence of God (*sic vere est*). Of course in this closely defined way existence is being asserted of the God described by *quo maius cogitari nequit*. And not only in this way, as *Prosl.* 2 showed. But in this definite manner only of God. This second definition reads—he does not only exist; there is no possibility of his being conceived as not existing. We might object (and the reason why *Prosl. 3* is frequently overlooked or taken lightly may be implicitly based on this objection), that this second statement that is now to be proved is identical with the first statement that was proved in *Prosl. 2*; in so far as this is accepted as proved. If the existence of God is proved there, then it must mean that it is impossible for him to be conceived as not existing. The antithesis between a God who exists only in thought and One who exists objectively (and therefore genuinely) as well as in thought showed—God would not be God if this 'God' who exists only in thought were God. We are not thinking of the true God when we think of this God. Thus it is impossible for us to conceive of the true God as not existing. To what extent is the thesis of *Prosl. 3* more than a mere repetition or underlining of this result from *Prosl. 2*?

Answers: in *Prosl. 2* the concept of existence was expressly the general concept of existence in thought and in reality. On that basis it was proved that it is impossible to conceive of God if his existence in thought and in reality are denied. But the very impossibility of thus denying the existence of a being can be understood as a merely factual denial that accompanies a recognition of this being's existence in fact, though insisting that in theory it might be possible for it not to exist. What we know as existing *in intellectu et in re* we cannot in fact at the same time conceive as not existing. But we cannot deny that we could think of it in itself as not existing (assuming that the factual impossibility would not hinder us). In *Prosl. 2* it was then shown that in actual fact God cannot be conceived as not existing. Not of course on the ground of positive knowledge of his existence. With the existence of God there is absolutely no question at all of a knowledge of his Existence such as we can have of the existence of other things, and the knowledge of it that we certainly have from revelation, was definitely eliminated here as a basis of proof. But on the basis of the revealed Name of God, which cannot possibly apply to a being that does not exist *in intellectu et in re*, the question arises of the God who exists *in intellectu et in re* and who, as bearer of this Name, is known only by revelation. Whoever hears and understands this Name can in fact apply this Name to no mere object of thought but only to the God who makes known his Existence in the same revelation. To that extent it is actually already proved in *Prosl. 2* that it is impossible for us to conceive the true God as not existing. However, it has not so far been proved, and the question now arises, whether it is true that the reason that prevents the actual denial of the Existence of God can also debar even the hypothetical conception of the non-existence of God. Could this reason not be of the same type as our positive acquaintance of the existence of other things on the ground of the knowledge that we have of them? This acquaintance certainly has the power to render impossible for us the thought that these things do not exist but it does not have the power to withhold from us the thought that their non-existence might be conceived. The concept of existence assumed in *Prosl. 2* is the general concept, applicable to all things that exist. A thing that we know as existing cannot at one and the same ·time be conceived as both existing and as not existing. But we can quite well conceive, simultaneously with the thought of its existence, that it possibly might not exist were it not known to us as existing. The question is now: whether, despite the proof just demonstrated, we are in such a position in respect of God that, knowing his existence, we have to reckon at the same time at least hypothetically with his non-existence or whether God makes an exception in the case of knowledge of his existence so that the knowledge that we have of him renders impossible in practice not only the thought of his non-existence, but also —likewise in practice—the thought of the very possibility of his non-existence. Must this impossibility in practice mean also the absolute exclusion of our conceiving God's non-existence? Our chapter answers this question. It lifts the concept of the Existence of God right out of the plane of the general concept of existence.[1] The limitation on the concept of existence— *esse in intellectu et in re*—with which it was applied to God in *Prosl. 2*, now disappears. Our chapter affirms the exception that is made here: the revealed Name of God has more power than the positive knowledge that we can have of the existence of other things *in intellectu et in re*. It compels in him who hears and understands it a recognition not only of the actual impossibility of the thought that God does not exist but also of the impossibility of that thought ever being conceived. Beyond the recognition that God exists, the Name of God as it is heard and understood compels the more precise definition that God does not exist as all other things exist whose non-existence we cannot reject in theory even when this theory is impossible for us to conceive in practice. But God exists—and he alone—

---

[1] C. in this respect: B. Adlhoch, '*Der Gottesbeweis des heiligen Anselm*' (*Philos. Jahrb. der Görresgesellschaft* vol. 8, Part 1 1895, pp. 380); K. Heim, *Das Gewissheitsproblem*, 1911, pp. 78; R. Seeberg, *Dogmengeschichte* vol. 3, 1913, pp. 150f; A. Koyré: *L'idée de Dieu, etc.*, 1923, pp. 193f.

in such a way that it is impossible even to conceive the possibility of his non-existence. That is the thesis of *Prosl. 3*. And that is not a repetition but a vital narrowing of the result of *Prosl. 2*.

At this point we insert an account of the essence of Gaunilo's comments on *Prosl. 3* that were put into *Pro insip. 7*[1] and also of Anselm's reply given in *C. Gaun. 4*. Gaunilo's objection is important because it is in it that his own position becomes relatively clearer than anywhere else. And Anselm's reply ought to be the best proof that the interpretation that we have just attempted of *Prosl. 3* is correct.

Leaving everything else aside, Gaunilo's main objection is to the whole manner in which the chapter puts the question. Instead of 'God cannot be conceived as not existing' (*cogitari*), on his view Anselm would have been better to have said, 'we cannot know God as not existing or as possibly not existing' (*intelligi*). Thereby denial of or doubt as to God's existence would be characterized as *falsum*, as Gaunilo thinks it ought to be. For *falsa nequeunt intelligi*: knowledge is ever knowledge of truth. However, that *falsa* and therefore also this particular *ialsum* can be conceived, as is obviously the case with the *fnsipiens*, Anselm had no intention of disputing. From this point onwards—just from the point where in its own way it becomes interesting—Gaunilo's exposition becomes sketchy:

'I know myself as existing and also at the same time as possibly not existing. On the other hand, I know God as existing but it is impossible for me to know him as possibly not existing. In knowing myself as existing, can I at the same time conceive of myself as not existing? I do not know.

[1] What is not of the essence is the repetition of the objection that the *rei veritate esse* of God must be made known or must have been made known in the first place otherwise than by means of the mere expression, before any sort of conclusions about his Existence can be drawn from the Perfection of God that the expression declares (I 129, 1–10). Gaunilo's confusion between *maius omnibus* and *quo maius cogitari nequit* (see pp. 84ff, above) has a particularly disastrous effect here—he actually paraphrases here Anselm's alleged *maius omnibus* with *natura maius et melius omnium quae sunt* and with *summa res*.

If I can then I can also do it for everything else whose existence I know with the same certainty. If I cannot, then the fact that I cannot conceive an existence as not existing is not true only in respect of God.'[1]

We see here (apart from the general statement in the last chapter this is the only occasion in his essay, but here it is very definite), that even Gaunilo asserts the existence of God, indeed the *intelligere* of the existence of God, though of course we also see at once that what he understands by it is something quite different from what Anselm understands. His *intelligere* is synonymous with a *scire* which for some reason or another is a *certissime scire*.[2] It may be that what he wants this to describe, if it is a case of *intelligere Deum esse*, is the same as Anselm describes[3] as the certainty of faith that is already well established prior to all theology. But perhaps he is familiar rather with the *certissimum argumentum* which he is always missing in Anselm and what he has in mind is some empirical knowledge of God, perhaps somewhat in the manner in which Thomas Aquinas later made it credible to many. Certainly he wants to be sure that his *intelligere* is understood differently from all pure thinking and *vice versa*, pure thinking also—of course to its shame—as independent from what he styles *intelligere*. Gaunilo 'recognizes' or 'knows' not a little: he knows, for example, even *certissime*, that he himself exists. He certainly also knows the limited nature of this his existence and therefore of the possibility of his non-existence. On the other hand he does not know—and he does not want to make up his mind merely 'by thinking'—whether despite this his knowledge of his existence

---

[1] *Cum autem dicitur, quod summa res ista non esse nequeat cogitari: melius fortasse diceretur, quod non esse aut etiam posse non esse non possit intelligi. Nam secundum propriet-atem verbi istius (sc. intelligere) falsa nequeunt intelligi, quae possunt utique eo modo cogitari, quo Deum non esse insipiens cogitavit. Et me quoque esse certissime scio, sed et posse non esse nihilominus scio; summum vero illud, quod est, scilicet Deus, et esse et non esse non posse indubitanter intelligo. Cogitare autem me non esse quamdiu esse certissime scio, nescio utrum possim; sed si possum, cur non et quidquid aliud eadem certitudine scio? Si autem non possum: non erit iam istud proprium Deo* (Pro insip. 7: I 129, 10ff).

[2] With this the passage cf. also *Pro insip.* 2 (I 125, 20ff): *. . . quia scilicet non possim hoc aliter cogitare nisi intelligendo id est scientia comprehendendo re ipsa illud existere.*

[3] Cf. pp. 26ff.

he could or could not conceive of himself as not existing. His position in respect of God is exactly the same. He knows God as existing and indeed even that it is impossible for him not to exist. But one sentence expressing this (perhaps on the ground of tradition, perhaps of experience or perhaps of both) would satisfy his claim to characterize the opposition of the *insipiens* as *falsum*. Against which he expects nothing from a special effort of thought in this realm (perhaps in any realm). Normally *cogitare* is just the simple reproduction of *intelligere*, and *intelligere* means *scire*. On the other hand (abnormal) thinking that is not identical with the reproduction of the thing known seems to him in all circumstances to be hopeless: just as much when it asserts (with Anselm) the Existence of God as when (with the *insipiens*) it denies it. Do I exist? Does anything exist? Does God exist? What thinking could decide these conclusively? Be my knowledge in all these points ever so sure, pure thinking as such is here as free as it is insufficient to make this decision. We can conceive of God as not existing.[1] Let us then abide by the thinking that is identical with the reproduction of knowledge.[2] The end of the passage is particularly remarkable. What does the 'either—or' mean with which Gaunilo ends? The question as to the necessity of the thought of his own existence was obviously dragged into the discussion because he assumed that behind Anselm's doctrine of the impossibility of the thought of God's non-existence there stood a general doctrine of necessary thoughts ultimately based on that of the necessity of his own existence. In my opinion he regarded him as standing where Descartes later stood. And so he thinks Anselm has only this alternative: either his statement 'the thought of one's own existence is necessary' is false—in which case all corresponding

---

[1] Thomas Aquinas (*Summa contra gentiles I 11*) will not be afraid to say later *nullum inconviens accidit ponentibus Deum non esse.*

[2] Bouchitté (*Le rationalisme chrétien*, p. 306), is no doubt right to compliment Gaunilo, admittedly in connection with a different passage, with the remark: *Les hommes accoutumés aux études philosophiques reconnaîtront certainement, qu'il y a dans ce passage et dans ce qui suit quelque chose que ne désavouerait pas la philosophie expérimentale et sensualiste de nos jours.*

statements collapse with it, including the statement, 'the thought of God's existence is necessary'. Or this statement is correct—in which case the statement about the existence of God has at least a parallel and that finishes the uniqueness of the Existence of God which Anselm asserted. It can be maintained that these last words of his, Gaunilo's polemic, are the most spiritually valuable in his whole work, and yet they are the least relevant to Anselm.

Anselm replied to this as follows. Just because the point at issue is the proof of the existence which is peculiar to God, our thesis must be: 'God cannot be conceived as not existing.' It is certainly true that God cannot be known as not existing, since a *falsum* can never be an object of knowledge. But supposing he, Anselm, had put forward this thesis, would Gaunilo not have replied to him (and correctly) in the sense of his closing sentence: this statement is applicable to all that exists and not only to God.[1] Whereas the statement, 'God cannot be conceived as not existing', can only have one subject, 'God'. For all that exists apart from God can be conceived as not existing.[2] The proof of this follows from the Nature of God.[3] All things finite and divisible (but only these) can be conceived as not existing: in view of what is beyond their spatial and temporal limits, in view of their partial non-identity with themselves, obviously the thought of their possible non-existence must occur, however assured we may be that their existence is known.[4] The Infinite and Indivisible, which is God (and it alone), cannot be conceived as not existing (in so far as on other

---

[1] *Si enim dixissem, rem ipsam non posse intelligi non esse, fortasse tu ipse . . . obiceres, nihil quod est posse intelligi non esse . . . Quare non esse proprium Deo non posse intelligi non esse (C. Gaun. 4:* 1 133, 24ff).

[2] *Sed hoc utique non potest obici de cogitatione, si bene consideretur. Nam et si nulla, quae sunt, possint intelligi non esse, omnia tamen possunt cogitari non esse praeter id quod summe est (ibid.:* 1 133, 29–134, 2).

[3] Once again it ought to be noted (cf. p. 97, n. 1, above) that the point here is not the actual question of the Existence of God, a question which is assumed to be still open, but the question as to what 'existence' can and does mean when it refers to God. This question is to be answered from the Nature of God.

[4] *Illa quippe omnia et sola possunt cogitari non esse, quae initium aut finem aut partium habent coniunctionem (ibid.:* 1 134, 2f).

grounds it must be conceived as existing). In so far as it has no bounds and in its totality is identical with itself, its existence (assuming it to possess such) cannot be denied.[1] Thus: if the Existence of God is to be proved then it must be proved that he cannot be conceived as not existing. But Anselm has no intention of relating this to any analogous statement about his own existence, let alone of setting it in a relation of dependence on such a statement, as Gaunilo seems to take for granted. There is no analogous statement (Anselm is not Descartes) concerning man's own existence. Of course Gaunilo can say that he does not know whether he could conceive himself as not existing while knowing his existence. Naturally he is able to do that as certainly as he is capable of creating a fiction by ignoring what he knows of his existence. The nature of man as distinct from the Nature of God will not put any obstacle in the way of such a fiction.[2] Anything at all (except God) we can conceive as not existing: that is to say, although we know its existence and although in fact we are not able to grasp the thought of its non-existence, we can create the hypothesis or fiction that would correspond.[3] Thus in reply to Gaunilo's sceptical statement that he does not know whether he could conceive himself as not existing, it has to be said that in actual fact he cannot do this (prevented by knowledge of his existence), but can do it very well hypothetically, as a fiction. And the same is true of our thinking in respect of all things apart from God.[4] Thus there is no general doctrine of necessary thoughts standing behind the thesis of *Prosl. 3*. That there are also things other

[1] *Illud vero solum non potest cogitari non esse, in quo nec initium nec finem nec partium coniunctionem, et quod non nisi semper et ubique totum ulla invenit cogitatio (ibid.: 1 134, 4ff).*

[2] *Scito igitur, quia potes cogitare te non esse, quamdiu esse certissime scis; quod te miror dixisse nescire. Multa namque cogitamus non esse, quae scimus esse, et multa esse, quae non esse scimus—non existimando sed fingendo ita esse ut cogitamus (ibid.: 1 134, 7ff).*

[3] *Et quidem possumus cogitare aliquid non esse quamdiu scimus esse, quia simul et illud possumus et istud scimus; et non possumus cogitare non esse quamdiu scimus esse, quia non possumus cogitare esse simul et non esse (ibid.: 1 134, 10ff).*

[4] *Si quis igitur sic distinguat huius prolationis has duas sententias, intelliget nihil, quamdiu esse scitur, posse cogitari non esse, et quidquid est praeter id quo maius cogitari nequit, etiam cum scitur esse, posse non esse cogitari (ibid., 1 134, 13ff).*

than God that cannot in fact be conceived as not existing, is a different matter. What is represented by Anselm in *Prosl. 3* is this sentence, of which God alone can be the subject: even in this second sense, even hypothetically, God cannot be conceived as not existing.[1] Anselm comes to terms in *Prosl. 4* with the fact, dealt with so disastrously by Gaunilo, that none the less the *insipiens* asserts that he can conceive the non-existence of God.[2] What had to be shown here was that in *Prosl. 3* Anselm is concerned with a problem which for all his vaunted positivism Gaunilo has not yet even seen. Just here, where Gaunilo is at his cleverest, all that he can show is that he is completely at cross purposes with Anselm for the reason that where his work ends, Anselm's begins.

Nam potest cogitari esse aliquid, quod non possit cogitari non esse; quod maius est, quam quod non esse cogitari potest. (I 102, 6ff)	It is possible to conceive as existing something which cannot be conceived as not existing: that which is greater than what can be conceived as not existing.

What follows now is the narrowing of the proof in *Prosl. 2* achieved in the sense of the opening sentence that sets the theme of the chapter. It is taken as proved and admitted that existence in general, *esse in intellectu et in re*, applies to God; on the other hand the special brand of true existence, applicable only to him (his *sic vere esse*) and which according to the opening sentence consists in the fact, not yet established in the proof, that he so exists that he cannot be conceived as not existing—that is taken as still open to question. Just because it is not a case of a second proof (nor indeed of a repetition of the first) but rather a case of narrowing the one and only proof, admittedly in a way that is decisive, without further preparation this narrowing is combined with the first general state-

---

[1] *Sic igitur et proprium est Deo non posse cogitari non esse, et tamen multa non possunt cogitari, quamdiu sunt, non esse (ibid.: I 134, 16ff).*

[2] *Quomodo tamen dicatur cogitari Deus non esse, in ipso libello puto sufficienter esse dictum (ibid.: I 134, 18f).*

ment; it can and must be essentially the same proof as before, except that now right along the line a second reflection on the impossibility of the non-existence of God is to be carried to the length of the impossibility of even conceiving his non-existence.

Anselm starts from the possibility of conceiving a being who exists and who cannot be thought together of as not existing and one who likewise exists but can be thought of as not existing. The *esse in intellectu et in re* in the sense of *Prosl.* 2 applies to both; but they are distinguished from one another in that theoretical denial of this *esse* is impossible in the case of the first being but possible in the case of the second. The opening statement is thus: these two beings and their existing side by side are conceivable.

Let us suppose that we did conceive of these two beings alongside one another. We must admit that once more we have conceived first of a 'greater' and of a 'smaller' being, a being of a higher and of a lower order. The principle of progressive orders which Anselm here assumes could be the same as that in *Prosl.* 2 only that this time we have a higher degree within the same series. It is now no longer a contrast between something that exists on the one hand merely in thought and on the other hand in thought and objectively but a contrast between something that certainly exists objectively as well as in thought but yet which is conceivable as not existing and on the other hand something existing objectively and in thought but which is not conceivable as not existing. Out of the general *vere esse* there now rises significantly before us a *vere esse* whose reality has its basis neither merely subjectively nor merely subjectively and objectively but is based beyond this contrast *a se*, in itself. A being to which *vere esse* in this latter sense applies, whose existence is therefore independent of the antithesis between knowledge and object, such a being is obviously a *maius*. It belongs to a higher level of existence than a being to which *vere esse* applies merely in the general sense, which however genuinely it may exist, is subject to this antithesis and whose existence can therefore be denied in theory by the same thinking as has to assert its existence in fact. This first being exists not only in reality but exists as the reality of existence itself, as the criterion of all existence and non-existence which is always presupposed in all thinking of the existence and non-existence of other beings; consequently it cannot be conceived as not existing. Whoever thinks of these two beings side by side has conceived this 'greater' over against a 'smaller'.

Quare si id quo maius nequit cogitari, potest cogitari non esse: id ipsum quo maius cogitari nequit non est id quo maius cogitari nequit; quod convenire non potest.

(I 102, 8ff)

When, therefore, 'that than which a greater cannot be conceived' can be conceived as not existing, then 'that than which a greater cannot be conceived' is not 'that than which a greater cannot be conceived'. Which is a contradiction.

For the sake of argument God is identified with this second being, who though existing, is however conceivable as not existing. Why should God not exist within this limitation as is the case with all other beings known to us? As the most exalted Being in the universe at the head of many others? The gods of the heathen seem to manage it. But that very fact raises the question whether these 'gods' justify their name. It is by the revelation of the Name of God that this question is decided. The God who is revealed is called *quo maius cogitari nequit.* And from that we again have this intolerable contradiction: this God who though existing can be conceived as not existing, is called *id quo maius cogitari nequit* and yet is not that. That a *maius* is conceivable has just been shown. *Quod convenire non potest.* Once again it is obvious that a pseudo-God has to be unmasked and the Name of God denied to a being who cannot be seriously taken as God. Whether or not this 'God' exists *in intellectu et in re,* he does not exist as God. God cannot possibly exist merely thus. In order to be identical with God, over and above his identity with a being who exists in this manner, he would have to be identical to this conceivable *maius.* Whether distinct from or similar to this latter he shows himself up for what he always is—not God.

Sic ergo vere est aliquid quo maius cogitari non potest, ut nec cogitari possit non esse (I 103, 1f)	Therefore 'something beyond which nothing greater can be conceived' exists in reality in such a manner that it cannot be conceived as not existing.

Again the conclusion is drawn: what is described as *aliquid quo maius cogitari non potest* exists in such a way that it cannot be conceived as not existing. To what extent is this conclusion binding? Clearly first of all, we repeat, only in so far as a 'God' conceivable as not existing is not disqualified from being God by the contradiction between the Name of the God who is revealed and the manner of existence of this so-called 'God'. God as he is revealed cannot in any circumstances exist in that way. But once more the actual conclusion stretches out beyond this negative that can be proved; from the impossibility of the revealed God having such an existence a conclusion is drawn as to the existence that is peculiar to him and which no thinking can question. And again it has to be said: this last, vital positive statement appears (after the opposite statement about God's existence being questioned by thinking has been proved absurd), without its following as a consequence from the preceding line of thought. It is brought in as a possibility of thought alongside another (*potest cogitari esse aliquid . . .*). If it is to remain, if it is now supposed to be proved, *sic ergo vere est*, then this can make sense only if an article of faith, fixed in itself as such, has been proved in such a way that the opposite statement would be reduced *ad absurdum* by means of the statement of the Name of God which is likewise assumed to be revealed and believed. This article of faith (regarding that existence of God which is not only genuine but also incapable of being denied even theoretically) was introduced first of all disguised as a possibility of thought alongside another, and it remains before us as the positive result after this opposite statement has been dropped. Responsibility for the givenness of this statement (for the last *ratio quomodo sit*)[1] is not for the

[1] Cf. pp. 27f.

theologian to bear. *Intelligere* means to see into the noetic rationality and therefore into the noetic necessity of the statements that are revealed, on the basis that they possess ontic rationality and necessity as revealed statements, prior to all *intelligere*, to all 'proof' and therefore not based on proof. This can only happen in theology as such. But it can happen and it is what in fact has happened here.

Before following *Prosl. 3* to its climax, for the sake of completeness we must turn once again to Anselm's Apology against Gaunilo. As already mentioned, in one passage there he plainly repeated the simple proof of *Prosl. 2*.[1] On the other hand, in a whole succession of passages—a further indication of where his interests lay—he continually offered his opponent new variations of the narrowed-down proof of *Prosl. 3*. We summarize them shortly so as to show: 1. That the decisive thought of *Prosl. 3* is not bound to the form which it is given there but is capable of variations; 2. that what these passages in fact deal with are variations of the narrowed-down proof of *Prosl. 3*.

1. *C. Gaun. 9*.[2] We start with this last passage because it is here that we find ourselves nearest to the form which the argument takes in *Prosl. 3*. Again, something that is conceived as 'greater' is compared with something conceived as 'smaller'. Again, the Name of God shows that God cannot be identical with this 'smaller'. And finally it is again taken to follow (on the basis of the so-called article of faith)—as he cannot be the 'smaller', God is the 'greater'. The difference between this and the basic form of *Prosl. 3* consists in the fact that here the *maius*

---

[1] *C. Gaun. 2:* 1 132, 22ff.

[2] *Palam autem est, quia similiter potest cogitari et intelligi, quod non potest non esse. Maius vero cogitat qui hoc cogitat, quam qui cogitat quod possit non esse. Dum ergo cogitatur quo maius non possit cogitari: si cogitatur quod possit non esse, non cogitatur quo non possit cogitari maius. Sed nequit idem simul cogitari et non cogitari. Quare qui cogitat quo maius non possit cogitari: non cogitat quod possit, sed quod non possit non esse. Quapropter necesse est esse quod cogitat, quia quidquid non esse potest, non est quod cogitat* (1 138, 19ff).

is defined as the *quod non potest non esse* and that in consequence the result must also be: *necesse est esse quod cogitat (sc. qui cogitat quo maius cogitari nequit)*. This distinction obviously involves an abbreviation; for rationality necessity is at once substituted, surely intimating—the proof consists in demonstrating that it is impossible to conceive of God as not existing.

2. *C. Gaun. 3.*[1] Here Anselm replies to Gaunilo's island analogy: what is described as *quo maius cogitari nequit* could not be conceived as not existing because it exists (if at all) in virtue of the rationality (and therefore on the basis) of Truth itself. If it did not exist thus it would not exist at all. The island analogy is nonsense because it overlooks the fact that it is only the existence of God (and therefore not the existence of this island) that can be proved as Anselm has proved it. And the argument proceeds: anyone who denies the existence of God must face the question whether he is really thinking of him who is called *quo maius cogitari nequit*. If he is not thinking of him then obviously he does not deny his existence. If he is thinking of him then he is thinking of one whose existence cannot be denied. For could his existence be denied then he would have to be conceivable as finite. But he is not conceivable as finite. (Whoever thinks of him who is called *quo maius cogitari nequit* is never to think of a finite being, but rather *ratione veritatis*, and so of a being that does not exist in the manner of finite beings). Therefore, whoever thinks of him thinks of one whose existence cannot be denied. Thus the existence of him who is called *quo maius cogitari nequit* cannot be denied. Here too we immediately recognize the nerve of the proof of *Prosl. 3*: by what his Name forbids, God is fundamentally

---

1 *Palam autem iam videtur, 'quo non valet cogitari maius' non posse cogitari non esse, quod tam certa ratione veritatis existit. Aliter enim nullatenus existeret. Denique si quis dicit se cogitare illud non esse, dico quia cum hoc cogitat: aut cogitat aliquid quo maius cogitari non possit, aut non cogitat. Si non cogitat, non cogitat non esse quod non cogitat. Si vero cogitat, utique cogitat aliquid quod nec cogitari possit non esse. Si enim posset cogitari non esse, cogitari posset habere principium et finem. Sed hoc non potest. Qui ergo illud cogitat, aliquid cogitat quod nec cogitari non esse possit. Hoc vero qui cogitat, non cogitat idipsum non esse. Alioquin cogitat, quod cogitari non potest. Non igitur potest cogitari non esse 'quo maius nequit cogitari'* (I 133, 10ff).

distinguished from all beings that can be conceived as not existing. The proof of course cannot establish that even when we deny his existence we still conceive of him and therefore must conceive of him in this his uniqueness as the infinite Being and therefore as existing. All it tries to prove and all it can prove is that when we really conceive him we conceive him as existing of necessity, as so existing that he cannot be conceived as not existing. This reminder of God's infinity alludes to one of the statements of revelation about the Nature of God. But the fact that God is infinite does not prove that he exists. Rather the fact that God is infinite proves that (if he exists) he exists differently from beings who are not infinite— that is, he does not exist in such a way that his existence can be denied. The positive conclusion that he exists does not follow from the statement quoted here concerning his Nature. That remains outstanding at the point where he who is called *quo maius cogitari nequit* is conceived and where therefore his existence too is an article of faith.

3. *C. Gaun. 1* (where Anselm gives the proof successively in three different forms). We are confronted first of all[1] with an inversion of the form just given under 2. He who is called *quo maius cogitari nequit* can be conceived as existing. But who is it who is then conceived? A being whose existence is infinite. A being whose existence could be denied would have to be conceived as a finite being. If then he who is called *quo maius cogitari nequit* is not conceivable as a finite being then his existence cannot be denied. If he can be conceived as existing, then of necessity he must exist, and that means he must be conceived as existing of necessity. Of the 'abbreviation' that is applied, the same is to be said as under 1; of the appeal to the infinity of God, the same as under 2. For the rest we again recognize the basic form—separation of God's existence from

---

[1] *Si vel cogitari potest esse, necesse est illud esse. Nam 'quo maius cogitari nequit' non potest cogitari esse nisi sine initio. Quidquid autem potest cogitari esse et non est, per initium potest cogitari esse. Non ergo 'quo maius cogitari nequit' cogitari potest esse et non est. Si ergo cogitari potest esse, ex necessitate est* (I 131, 1ff).

that of all other beings. Consequently, this existence, unlike that of all other beings, cannot be disputed. Conclusion (the positive article of faith remains outstanding): God exists of necessity.

4. *C. Gaun. 1* in a second passage:[1] Anselm takes as his starting-point the assumption that at least the concept as such expressed in the Name *quo maius cogitari nequit* (no matter whether the existence of its bearer is accepted or denied) is capable of realization. Supposing then someone were to deny or doubt his Existence, that man could nevertheless neither deny nor doubt that if he, who bears this name, did exist in accordance with his Name then he would have to exist and that with ontic objectivity (*actu*) as much as for our knowledge (*intellectu*). His Name forbids that he should be reckoned as one of those beings who merely exist in fact, that is who are recognized as existing. A purely conceptual being and one that does not really exist could never be obliged to exist: even if it did exist it could obviously either exist or not exist, be known as existing or as not existing; at best it would be a being existing in fact and known as existing. The 'if then' statement is therefore not applicable to a purely conceptual being that does not really exist but only to a being who can be conceived and who really does exist, of whom at the same time it can be said what is in fact to be said of God: it is impossible for it not to exist or to be conceived as not existing. A highly complicated feature, but one that is very significant for Anselm's thought and intention in this matter, is that at first the question as to the general existence of God (in the sense of *Prosl. 2*) is expressly left open. It is only the Name of God that is introduced by the hypothesis: *cogitari potest*. Then the Name of God extorts the admission that he who has this Name, if he existed (in the sense of *Prosl.*

---

1 *Amplius. Si utique vel cogitari potest, necesse est illud esse. Nullus enim negans aut dubitans esse aliquid quo maius cogitari non possit, negat vel dubitat quia, si esset, nec actu nec intellectu potest non esse. Aliter namque non esset quo maius cogitari non posset. Sed quidquid cogitari potest et non est: si esset, posset vel actu vel intellectu non esse. Quare si vel cogitari potest, non potest non esse 'quo maius cogitari nequit'* I 131, 6ff).

2), would exist of necessity (in the sense of *Prosl. 3*). Then this 'if' is whittled down by the assertion that a purely conceptual being, even if it did exist (in the sense of *Prosl. 2*), would not exist of necessity. And then it is concluded (we would have appreciated a transitional step)—God is no mere conceptual being but one who exists in the *Prosl. 2* sense, that is one who exists of necessity. The procedure is then—first the question of *Prosl. 3* is answered hypothetically and then by means of this hypothetical answer (!) the question of *Prosl. 2*, and, following from it, the question of *Prosl. 3*, are answered categorically.

5. And now in a third passage[1] of *C. Gaun. 1*, Anselm goes yet a step further. The question of *Prosl. 2* is to be taken not just as being open, but as being denied, apart from the possibility of conceiving the thought-content of God's Name. Again two 'if then' statements of similar content now appear but in reverse order from that in the form given previously: if a purely conceptual being not really existing were to exist, then as such (for obviously even if it were a being that existed it would not be one that existed of necessity) it would not be identical to God. Therefore, if God were to exist as such a merely conceptual being not really existing, then he would not be identical with himself. Therefore, this hypothesis is absurd. Therefore, in conceiving the thought-content of this Name, all we can assume is the existence of its bearer. The Name of God thus demands that his existence, even if it is denied, cannot (and incidentally this renders its denial impossible) be conceived merely as an existence in fact, but only as one that is necessary.

6. *C. Gaun. 5*[2] is worked out with the same material. Again

---

[1] *Sed ponamus non esse, si vel cogitari valet. At quidquid cogitari potest et non est: si esset, non esset 'quo maius cogitari non possit'. Si ergo esset 'quo maius cogitari non possit', non esset quo maius cogitari non possit; quod nimis est absurdum. Falsum est igitur non esse aliquid quo maius cogitari non possit, si vel cogitari potest* (I 131, 12ff).

[2] *Nam quod non est, potest non esse; et quod non esse potest, cogitari potest non esse. Quidquid autem cogitari potest non esse: si est, non est quo maius cogitari non possit. Quod si non est: utique si esset, non esset quo maius non possit cogitari. Sed dici non potest, quia 'quo maius non possit cogitari' si est, non est quo maius cogitari non possit; aut si esset, non esset quo non possit cogitari maius. Patet ergo quia nec non est nec potest non esse aut cogitari non esse. Aliter enim si est, non est quod dicitur; et si esset, non esset* (I 134, 31–135, 7).

the hypothesis is on the one hand the non-existence of God and on the other, the conceivability of his Name. From the first would follow the possibility of his non-existence and from the second its conceivability. However, something conceivable as not existing, even if it does exist, is not the legitimate bearer of the Name *quo maius cogitari nequit*. And if it does not exist, it would not be the legitimate bearer of this name, even if it were to exist, for alongside him there would be a Greater conceivable, who could not be conceived as not existing. This impossibility of regarding it as the legitimate bearer of the Name of God is the characteristic distinction between God and every being that is conceivable as not existing. Thus God would have to be a being distinct from himself in order to be a being conceivable as not existing. And so he cannot be a being conceivable as not existing. With the inconceivability of his non-existence, its very possibility also collapses and incidentally with it the reality of his non-existence that was the hypothesis.

In all six of these variants the object of the Proof (in agreement with *Prosl. 3*) is not the existence that God has in common with beings who are different from him, but rather that peculiar, indeed unique and in the end only true existence which, over and above this general existence, applies only to him—the absolutely necessary, because original existence *ratione veritatis*. Incidentally forms four to six reach conclusions that refer back to general existence and so to a strengthening of the Proof of *Prosl. 2*. But only incidentally. There can be no question but that in these last four forms too Anselm's primary and decisive interest was the *non cogitari potest non esse*. In all its six forms the Proof consists (again agreeing with *Prosl. 3*) in demonstrating: it is impossible to conceive him who is called *quo maius cogitari nequit* as existing in the way that other beings are conceivable as existing, that is in such a way that his non-existence could be conceived. His Name and his Nature exclude this. In demonstrating this the way is prepared for the positive statement: God so exists that his non-existence is inconceivable. This statement as such is not proved. On the contrary it stands, like the general statement of *Prosl. 2*, 'God exists', as an article of faith by itself. What happens in the Proof and its variants is that sometimes this article of faith is strictly proved, at other times its opposite is strictly excluded by the Proof, that is by the interpretation of the revealed Name and Nature · of God. That is the *intelligere* of God's Existence corresponding to Anselm's programme.

Et hoc es tu, Domine Deus noster. Sic ergo vere es, Domine Deus meus, ut nec cogitari possis non esse: et merito. Si enim aliqua mens posset cogitare aliquid melius te, ascenderet creatura super Creatorum et indicaret de Creatore, quod valde est absurdum.
(1 103, 3ff)

And this thou art, O Lord our God. Thou dost exist in truth in such a way that thou canst not be conceived as not existing. And that with reason. For if any and every mind were able to conceive of something better than thee then the creature would be rising above the Creator and judging the Creator. This would be most absurd.

Whether or not we understand this part of the text perhaps determines for every reader of Anselm whether the whole is understood or not. The chapter could have closed with the preceding sentence, for with that sentence the Proof as such is completed. But the chapter does not close and anyone who does not heed this, anyone who does not take what Anselm now inserts at least as seriously as the actual Proof will most certainly misunderstand the Proof itself. In the first place Anselm resumes the form of address to God, that is he passes from the language of theological inquiry to the language of prayer. Or rather—once again[1] he shows that the whole theological inquiry is intended to be understood as undertaken and carried through in prayer. In prayer and surely that means—by presupposing in the most positive manner conceivable the object of the

[1] Cf. the opening sentences of *Prosl. 2*.

inquiry, his Presence and his Authority for the course and the success of the inquiry concerning him. This 'object' who is worshipped and thus investigated is, however, *Dominus Deus noster* = *Dominus Deus meus*, the God who is Lord of the Church and as such is the God of the inquiring theologian, who is Lord in this double relationship and to whom only devout obedience is possible. Theology is devout obedience. Could Anselm interpret his *Credo ut intelligam* more clearly than by revealing this attitude in which he pursues his study and more obviously than by insisting that it is on this that the course and outcome of his inquiry depend? Even formally his inquiry is distinguished by a provocative lack of all doubt, including all 'philosophic doubt', of all anxiety, including all apologetic anxiety and in this connection by a no less provocative intellectual coolness. Can it be otherwise when theology is what it is for him: assent to a decision coming from its object, from the 'Lord', acknowledgment and recognition of the 'Lord's' own communication of himself? It is certain that we cannot take Anselm's attitude that is so manifest here as proof that his thinking is based on received revelation. But it does assuredly prove that he means his thinking to be thus based and it is in that way that he wants to be understood as a thinker. If anyone interprets his argument as an a-priori philosophical system then he will certainly not have support from Anselm himself at any point. Anselm's own words have to be quietly altered and abbreviated if he is to be so interpreted. Just as, for example, Anselm's critics, beginning with Gaunilo of Marmoutiers, have discreetly taken no notice of this passage and all that follows from it. We can interpret his Proof only when, along with Anselm, in Anselm's own sense, we share the presupposition of his inquiry—that the object of the inquiry stands over against him who inquires not as 'it', not even as 'he', but as 'thou', as the unmediated 'thou' of the Lord.—'And this thou art. . . .' 'That' refers to *aliquid quo maius cogitari non potest*. It was in fact the assumption made at the beginning of *Prosl. 2*—*Credimus te esse aliquid pro nihil maius cogitari possit.* Now at the end of the inquiry it is again brought to remembrance. It is not just of anything, but of God the Lord whom we believe because he has revealed himself because he stands unmediated over against us as God the Lord, it is of him that it is proved that he exists—since he exists thus: 'in truth', and that now means in such a way, 'that thou canst not be conceived as not existing'. He who is present in unmediated form to the thinking churchman and who is worshipped by him, he is the One whose existence cannot only be thought of as sure in itself, but in relation to him even thinking is not free; he renders impossible the very thought of his non-existence, so certainly is he the One 'beyond whom a greater cannot be conceived'. But this equation which is vital for the Proof in its general and special form, is it valid? Does God really bear this Name? Must everyone who conceives of God really conceive of the prohibition expressed in this Name? Anselm does subsequently establish this basis of the whole— theologically as is appropriate. There is an *intelligimus* that also corresponds to the *credimus* at the beginning of *Prosl. 2*. How do we know that God's real Name is *quo maius cogitari nequit*? We know it because that is how God has revealed himself and because we believe him as he has revealed himself. But this knowing can be explained: we know it because on the basis of revelation and faith, standing before God, we know that we do not stand as any one being before any other being, but as a creature before his Creator. As such, and from him who stands over against us, we do not fail to hear this Name of God and we unhesitatingly accept the prohibition it expresses. To what extent? To the extent that the creature stands absolutely under his Creator and remains there and therefore in his thinking cannot set anything above the Creator. Along with his existence, he also has his thinking about existence, its values and its degrees, all entirely from the Creator. His thinking can be true only in so far as it is true in the Creator himself. The conception of a 'better' beyond the Creator would imply for the creature an ascent (*ascendere*) to a point where by nature he cannot stand, a judgment (*iudicare*) by a standard of truth or value which by nature he cannot possess. Conceiving a greater than the Creator would therefore mean absurdity—not in the literal sense but the great logical-moral absurdity which just because it is that, cannot be. The Creator as such is absolutely the *quo maius cogitari nequit* for the creature as such. Should the creature fail to hear this Name of God and the prohibition it contains then that can only mean that he has not yet understood the Creator as such nor himself as creature. It is in faith that he understands him and himself within this relation and so hears his Name and the prohibition against conceiving anything greater than him.[1] And so Anselm, who has proved that

[1] We note here two further objections which Thomas Aquinas raised against the Proof of *Prosl. 3*. The first is given (*Sententiae lib. 1 Dist. 111 Qu. 1, Art 1 ad 4*: Daniels, p. 65) as Anselm's interpretation: *Ratio Anselmi ita intelligenda est: quod postquam intelligimus Deum, non potest intelligi quod sit Deus et possit cogitari non esse; sed tamen ex hoc non sequitur quod aliquis non possit negare vel cogitare Deum non esse; potest enim cogitare nihil huius modi esse quo maius cogitari non possit; et ideo ratio sua procedit ex hac suppositione, quod supponatur aliquid esse quo maius cogitari non potest.* This exposition is as unlike Anselm as it could possibly be and can only be taken as criticism. Of the exposition itself we can say: the view that God cannot be conceived as not existing does not in any circumstances follow for Anselm from an *a priori intelligere Deum*, but from the article of faith; 'God is called *quo maius cogitari nequit*', just as insight into this article of faith follows in its turn from the article of faith 'God is the Creator'. In Anselm *aliquid esse quo maius cogitari non potest* is not a *suppositio* but the revelation apart from which there is no theology at all. In this case it is the revelation of the Name of God and of the prohibition which it expresses. This prohibition certainly 'can' be transgressed. We 'can' therefore *cogitare nihil huius modi esse quo maius cogitari non potest*. When Anselm says that we cannot conceive this he says it in the presence of God and therefore as one who cannot transgress this prohibition. In Thomas' criticism this sense of 'unable' is unfortunately disregarded. The second objection, now openly formulated as such, reads (*Summa contra gentiles 1 11*): *Nec etiam oportet. . . . Deo posse aliquid maius cogitari si potest cogitari non esse. Nam quod possit cogitari non esse, non ex imperfectione sui esse est vel incertitudine, cum suum esse sit secundum se manifestissimum, sed ex debilitate nostri intellectus, qui eum intueri non potest per seipsum sed ex effectibus eius.* We can compare with this the final words of *Prosl. 3* to catch a glimpse of the contradiction between two worlds that is disclosed here. When Anselm speaks of revelation and faith Thomas disputes the possibility of *intuitio Dei per seipsum*. So where Anselm sees *stultitia* and *insipientia* at work against the background of divine reprobation, where he sees God offended by the exaltation of the creature above the Creator (Cf. *C.D.h. I 15:* II 72, 29ff), the problem for Thomas is creaturely imperfection, to which he can reconcile himself by remembering the unassailable 'manifestness' of God *secundum se*, and by demonstrating the *intuitio Dei ex effectibus eius*.

it is impossible for him who is called *quo maius cogitari nequit* not to exist, can say with a clear conscience that he has proved it impossible for God not to exist.

Et quidem quidquid est aliud praeter te solum, potest cogitari non esse. Solus igitur verissime omnium et ideo maxime omnium habes esse: quia quidquid aliud est, non sic vere, et idcirco minus habet esse.

(I 103, 6ff)

And so it stands: whatever exists apart from thee, the Only One, can be conceived as not existing. Thou alone of all beings hast really true existence—and therefore thou alone of all beings hast perfect existence. For anything other than thee[1] does not possess this manner of existence and therefore possesses but imperfect existence.

Anselm has proved that it is impossible for God not to exist. That means, however, that he has proved what can be proved only of God. For that reason then the main point that Anselm wanted to make did not come till the narrowed-down Proof of *Prosl. 3* and it was not the general Proof of *Prosl. 2*. Of course in *Prosl. 2* he had also proved that God certainly did exist, that is possessed not just reality in thought but objective reality. But what a complete misunderstanding it is to think that this Proof formed the substance of his purpose! If God were to exist merely generally, in the manner of all other beings, then not only would he not exist as God, but according to Anselm's own account[2]—he did not create himself and therefore does not possess existence as such, as is granted to the creature—he would not exist at all. All that his Existence has in common with that of other beings is objective reality as such. But the objective reality of all beings apart from him is such that it can be conceived as not existing and indeed in a special sense has to be conceived as not existing. This to the extent that the existence of all beings apart from him is conditioned by his Existence and is an existence that is bestowed from out of his Existence. The reason why there is such a thing as existence is that God exists. With his Existence stands or falls the existence

[1] Koyré: *Tout ce qui n'est pas toi.*

[2] *Certa ratione veritatis existit; aliter enim nullatenus existeret (C. Gaun. 3: I 133, 11f).*

of all beings that are distinct from him. Only fools and their theological and philosophical supporters, the Gaunilos, could think that the criterion of general existence is the criterion of God's Existence and could therefore either not get beyond *Prosl. 2* or take *Prosl. 3* as conditioned by *Prosl. 2*. Whereas it is all the other way round: it is the Existence of God that is the criterion of general existence and if either of these two chapters of Anselm is ultimately or decisively conditioned by the other, then it is *Prosl. 2* by *Prosl. 3*, and not *vice versa*. It is the Existence of God that is proved when it is proved that God cannot be conceived as not existing. Thus, with the prohibition against conceiving anything greater than him and with this prohibition ruling out the thought of his non-existence— thus does God alone confront man. Thus he and he alone is objective reality. Because God exists in the inexplicable manner which thought cannot dismiss, as he does exist as bearer of his revealed Name, for that reason there is objective reality and the possibility of its being conceived and so there is also the possibility of conceiving of God as existing at all (in the sense of *Prosl. 2*). In which case absolutely everything that exists apart from him exists, as it were, coupled to his Existence and is therefore conceivable as existing only in relation to the conception of his Existence (that cannot be denied) and so, apart from this connection, is ever conceivable, also as non-existing. God alone is incapable of not existing and therefore he alone can be the subject of the Proof of *Prosl. 3*. Therefore the One and Only God—we cannot emphasize too strongly or take too seriously the fact that Anselm says all this in the second person singular—has Existence that is utterly true (*verissime*) and therefore perfect (*maxime*).

Vere est was how it was put in *Prosl. 2* and what was meant was quite generally that God has at least as much objective reality as all other beings. Then *Prosl. 3* qualified this thesis—*quod sic vere est, ut nec cogitari possit non esse*. But this same *sic* that does the qualifying also designates the truth of God's Existence as being different from that of the existence of all other beings: *verissime . . . habes esse.* The superlative (and we may equally well add even the superlative *maxime*) is a faltering phrase for the fusion of truth and appropriateness, applicable to all existence different from God himself if it is to be true and right; the fusion which also applies to *Prosl. 2*, to the existence of God himself; the fusion which according to *Prosl. 3* is identical with the insoluble but intellectually inevitable Existence of God as Creator. There are beings who exist. Even God is a Being who exists. But God alone, the Creator, is a being who exists in a manner insoluble but beyond the power of thought to deny, in relation to whom true and appropriate existence is also given to other beings. *Verissime* and *maxime,* in the truth and appropriateness which is the criterion of all existence, God alone has existence. While the *esse* and even the *vere esse* is not to be denied to these beings that are distinct from him who is inconceivable as not existing, nevertheless the *sic esse* or *sic vere esse,* the truth and appropriateness of their existence, come from God and remain in God. What God has in perfection (qualitative and not quantitative) they have only in imperfection (qualitative and not just quantitative)—Existence, objective reality. No one, nothing else at all confronts me as thou dost—in such a way that this *ascendere* above and *iudicare* on the object is made impossible for me and the only question is of obedience or disobedience. And so in fact (the result of the previous consideration of the Name of God is confirmed)—the Existence of God is proved when it is proved that God cannot be conceived as not existing.

Cur itaque 'dixit insipiens in corde suo: non est Deus', cum tam in promptu sit rationali menti te maxime omnium esse? Cur, nisi quia stultus et insipiens?	On what ground, then, did the fool say 'there is no God' when to the rational mind it is quite plain that thou of all beings dost exist in perfection? On what other ground than that he is perverse and foolish?
(I 103, 9ff)	

Anselm comes back to the starting-point of his inquiry. Alongside the believer, who in relation to the Existence of God now stands within appropriate limits as one who knows, there still stands, unmoved like a block of wood, the *insipiens* with his '*Non est Deus*'. The formal, inner necessity of the statement *est aliqua talis natura*[1] is demonstrated, but that does not create any necessity in fact to take it as a positive statement instead of as a question. Although, in fact just because, this demonstration was a self-contained circle, it is confronted (Anselm does not need any Gaunilo to say it) with the assertion, 'God is not a real object', with the same kind of consistency about it as presumably belongs to a self-enclosed circle. The analysis of this actual (physical) possibility of the thesis of unbelief (Anselm is certainly as passionately concerned with it as any Gaunilo) is treated as a special problem at the end of *Prosl. 4*. Here it concerns him—in complete contrast to the knowledge of faith that has been achieved—only as fact. He has not forgotten and has no intention of overlooking this other person who keeps on saying and is obviously able to say and perhaps is bound to say, '*Deus non est*'. He does not forget or overlook him just because he himself stands so very close to him and because by this opposition he himself is faced with the question which is now answered. *Unum idemque est quod quaerimus!* Did he not have to know his opponent's case very intimately and expound it very forcibly in order to defeat him and so raise faith to knowledge? Is not he, who obviously was so well able to conceive and expound this opposite point of view, himself in some way and at some point an *insipiens* too? Or at least is the solidarity between him and his opponent not so entirely broken that he could always understand him as well as he understands himself? It is enough that side by side with the man who says, 'only God really exists', there is the man who says on the other hand, 'there is no God'. And with him the question arises, 'Why does he talk thus? Where is he from? Who is he?' The question: *quomodo insipiens dixit* . . . of *Prosl. 4*[2] is not the same question. It is, as it were, a question as to the nature of the

---

[1] *Prosl. 2:* I 101, 6.   [2] I 103, 13.

negative statement. At the moment all that Anselm is concerned with is its reality as such (*cur?*). One possible reason that might lead a man to say, '*Deus non est*' is now rejected in accordance with the Proof just presented: he is no longer able to say that he cannot understand the article of faith on the Existence of God as such or the necessity of its content in relation to the other articles of faith. For the present all that could be done for such understanding, has been done—according to Anselm better results are admittedly in reserve. As a matter of fact 'sound human understanding' can tell us—not only that God exists, but that of all other beings he alone exists in perfection, *verissime, maxime*. It is certainly astonishing that Anselm ventures to describe denial of the Existence of God as a self-evident impossible possibility, for the *rationalis mens* simply excluded—in view of the possibility of theological instruction and especially in view of his theologoumenon just concluded which quite openly and admittedly was brought about with the help of very different material from 'sound human understanding'. And it is even more astonishing that after this reason has collapsed all that he appears to be able to consider is one other reason—divine reprobation of whoever denies the Existence of God. But if from false theological pride or with an unkind severity, anyone could argue against an earnestly seeking fellow mortal, once again the vital condition involved in Anselm's thinking would be ignored. We saw that this thinking is achieved—and this is the most important thing that can be said about it—as it continues in worship.[1] The subduing of the *mens rationalis* which he describes here as happening once for all, is for him the being subdued by the object, the *Dominus Deus noster*, before whose face he has been theologizing; the being subdued which he himself has experienced and which he can and must also assume to be the case with anyone who has been truly theologizing with him. According to

[1] Within the framework of the Benedictine *opus Dei*, ought perhaps to be added in order to be quite concrete.

Anselm there are no theological problems that are finally settled, so surely must we, when we have prayed, pray again and continue to pray. But it would be prayer devoid of faith in the hearing of prayer (and therefore not prayer) if theological thinking in the act of its fulfilment were not entirely sure of its case and so unwilling to venture forth at its own level with its unconditional demand. And it is exactly the same with the basis which Anselm describes as the only possible basis for the statement *Deus non est*. From what has been already said and in this whole context, the commonplace explanation of *quia stultus est et insipiens* is quite impossible—that the man who says *Deus non est* is a clown who is incapable of following the proof because he cannot think logically. That would be a completely unjustifiable affront to one's fellow mortal. Anselm comes nowhere near it: we will hear in *Prosl. 4* that he explained the meaning of the statement *Deus non est* entirely on the assumption that from the intellectual point of view he who holds it is to be taken seriously. Neither is any moral defect directly expressed by the *stultus et insipiens*. That it signifies both intellectual and moral perversity is of course undoubtedly true. Obviously the *stultus* inserted into the quotation reinforces the statement in this direction. And the point is not a perversity that is, as it were, physical but technical, and here again not a perversity of individual functions but of the whole position. The *insipiens* may be quite normal intellectually and morally. Only that, whether normal or not, he is just an *insipiens*; one who accomplishes what is not physically impossible but what it is forbidden to attempt; one who puts himself (the inner impossibility is not an outward impossibility for him) in a position where as a human being, normal or otherwise, he can only fall.[1] Anselm did not ascribe it to any quality of his

---

[1] *Volendo aliquid, quod velle tunc non debebat, deseruit iustitiam et sic peccavit (De casu diab. 4:* I 241, 4f). *Ideo illam deseruit, quia voluit quod velle non debuit; et hoc modo, id est volendo quod non debuit illam deseruit. Cur voluit quod non debuit? Nulla causa praecessit hanc voluntatem, nisi quia velle potuit. An ideo voluit, quia potuit? Non; quia similiter potuit velle bonus angelus; nec tamen voluit . . . Cur ergo voluit? Non nisi quia voluit. Nam*

own, but to the grace of God, that he himself was not an *insipiens* doing the same thing and that for him the inner impossibility was at the same time an outward one.[1] For that reason the otherwise fearful reproach, 'Thou art a *stultus et insipiens*', is not a direct reproach. It is only by the grace of God that Anselm's solidarity with him has been ended. The *insipiens* thinks and speaks as one who is not saved by the grace of God. That is the reason for his perversity, and why he can say, *Deus non est*. The reproach does not imply any uncharitableness. It is with just this reproach on his lips that Anselm takes his place as near as it is possible to be and therefore with as much promise as there could possibly be, alongside this fellow mortal whose action is so unintelligible. It is precisely with this reproach that, at the end of his attempt 'to prove' the article of faith about the existence of God, he has to declare

haec voluntas nullam aliam habuit causam . . . sed ipsa sibi efficiens causa fuit, si dici potest, et effectum (ibid. 27: I 275, 21ff). 'The actual origin of evil is for Anselm an "unfathomable" fact, that means one that is devoid of any inner or outer necessity' (F. R. Hasse, *Anselm von Canterbury* vol. 2, 1852, p. 427).

[1] *Utrum aliquis hanc rectitudinem non habens eam aliquo modo a se habere possit? Utique a se illam habere nequit, nisi aut volendo aut non volendo. Volendo quidem nullus valet eam per se adipisci, quia nequit eam velle, nisi illam habeat. Quod autem aliquis non habens rectitudinem voluntatis, illam valeat per se non volendo assequi, mens nullius accipit. Nullo igitur modo potest eam creatura habere a se. Sed neque creatura valet eam habere ab alia creatura. Sicut namque creatura nequit creaturam salvare, ita non potest illi dare per quod debeat salvari. Sequitur itaque quia nulla creatura rectitudinem habet . . . nisi per Dei gratiam . . . ita ut gratia sola possit hominem salvare, nihil eius libero arbitrio agente . . . dando voluntati rectitudinem quam servet per liberum arbitrium. Et quamvis non omnibus det, quoniam 'cui vult miseretur, et quem vult indurat': nulli tamen dat pro aliquo praecedenti merito, quoniam 'quis prior dedit Deo et retribuetur ei?' Si autem voluntas: . . . meretur aut augmentum acceptae iustitiae aut etiam potestatem pro bona voluntate aut praemium aliquod: haec omnia fructus sunt primae gratiae et 'gratia pro gratia'; et ideo totum est imputandum gratiae, 'quia neque volentis est' quod vult, 'neque currentis est' quod currit, 'sed miserentis est Dei'. Omnibus enim, excepto solo Deo, dicitur: 'Quid habes quod non accepisti? . . .' (De concordia Qu. III, 3: II 266, 8–267, 4). Scio . . . quod bona tua sicut fraude nulla tibi arripere aut auferre possum, sic nec ullis meritis obtinere me omnia posse quibus ad te revertar et complaceam. Quid enim meritis meis deberi potest, nisi mortis aeternae supplicium? Scio quod in beneplacito tuo sancto est me disperdere secundum multitudinem flagitiorium . . . vel reformare me, vel facere me tibi acceptabilem secundum divitias inaestimabiles misericordiae tuae, qui solus es reformator creaturae quam solus formasti (Medit. 7, 4: MPL 158, 744). Ad te confugio, sciens quod non est mihi fuga a te nisi ad te. Quis me potest liberare de manibus tuis, nisi tu solus? . . . Ad teipsum, obsecro, respice, cui nunquam sine veniae spe supplicatur. In temetipso invenies unde et propter quod miserearis secundum abundantiam suavitatis tuae et immensitatem misericordiae tuae. Noli, obsecro, ad me respicere, quia nihil in me invenies, nisi unde irasci debeas vel nisi morte aeterna dignissimum (ibid.: MPL 158, 744f).*

the possibility of a statement that contradicts it. This contradictory statement is the statement of unbelief, of the corrupt will, of man unreconciled.

3. THE POSSIBILITY OF DENYING THE EXISTENCE OF GOD (*Prosl. 4*)

Quomodo insipiens dixit in corde, quod cogitari non potest. (I 103, 13)	How the fool has said in his heart something that cannot be conceived.

For Anselm the problem of the man who denies God is first raised by the fact that he has designated as a 'fool' one who is where he is only by the wrath of God. He says in his heart what, according to the above proof, cannot be conceived at all. Only as an *insipiens* is he capable of this. Thus it is concluded that his statement is nonsense, must be nonsense and is debarred from serious theological debate. But this other statement, reached at the end of *Prosl. 3*, 'the fool has said in his heart, "There is no God" '—is also a statement of faith which as such requires knowledge. If the sense of the statement, 'God exists' is really to be understood then the nonsense of the opposite statement as such must be understood too. Anselm takes for the subject of a final inquiry not how the fool comes to be a fool—that is his secret and God's—but rather how the fool behaves as a fool, what constitutes the folly of denying the Existence of God and to what extent his statement is really nonsense which must be debarred from serious theological debate.

Verum quomodo dixit in corde quod cogitare non potuit; aut quomodo cogitare non potuit quod dixit in corde, cum idem sit dicere in corde et cogitare? (I 103, 14ff)	But how did he come to say in his heart what he cannot have conceived or how could he not conceive what he said in his heart, since 'to say in one's heart' and 'to conceive' are one and the same thing?

The question as to the foolishness of the fool may be put in two ways. The first way is to make his foolishness as such the starting-point. He says in his heart what he is unable to conceive.

He says, namely, 'God does not exist'. And according to the exposition in *Prosl. 3* that is something he cannot conceive. Not at all? But he nevertheless says it in his heart. Therefore, he can do the impossible. For obviously 'saying in his heart' and 'conceiving' are the same. Questions: How does he manage it? How can he reconcile this contradiction within himself? The other way is to make the fact of his foolishness the starting-point. He cannot conceive the thing that he says in his heart. What he says is, 'God does not exist'. But as has been shown, that is something he cannot conceive. But he still does it. Can he really not do it? Even where 'to say in his heart' and 'to conceive' are the same? Should he not therefore be able to say that his foolishness is not foolishness at all? Thus: 1. How far can he say what he can in no sense conceive? 2. How far can he conceive what he can in no sense say? This is the question of the foolishness of the fool that must be asked and answered if the fact of the denial of God is to be proved as a fact of foolishness and if the proof of God's Existence is thereby to be completed.

Quod si vere, immo quia vere et cogitavit quia dixit in corde, et non dixit in corde quia cogitare non potuit: non uno tantum modo dicitur aliquid in corde vel cogitatur. (I 103, 16ff)	If, or rather because he has actually conceived it (for he said it in his heart) and has not said it in his heart (for he could not conceive it) —it is clear that 'to say in one's heart' or 'to conceive' is not an unambiguous proceeding.

Despite the assumption that 'to say in one's heart' and 'to think' are one and the same thing, it might happen—in fact with the *insipiens* it actually does happen—that on the one hand someone in fact thinks something: he could do this; because he said it in his heart, he could therefore say it, could and did therefore also conceive it. And on the other hand, he did not say this in his heart: he could not do it; because he could not think it, he therefore could not say it and for that reason he did not say it. Thus: He did a thing and did not do it; he could do something and could not do it. This miracle is then only possible as a miracle of foolishness (and that it certainly is) if his 'saying in his heart' and his 'thinking' are different things, or to the extent that he can say and think a thing at the same time as he cannot say or think it. He does it and can do it in a different way (*non eodem modo—aliter* is what it is called later) from the way he cannot and does not do it. The assertion and the denial of the Existence of God do not take place—here we have the fundamental solution of the problem—on the same plane at all. The fool is able to say what he is certainly unable to conceive in so far as when he says it he is standing on a plane where he can assert the non-existence of God. And he is unable to conceive of what he is nevertheless able to say in so far as he is standing on another plane where it would be impossible for him to assert the non-existence of God. This is the fool's basic folly that in his thinking he is standing on a plane where the assertion of God's non-existence is certainly possible but where to stand on that plane is in itself—folly.

Aliter enim cogitatur res cum vox eam significans cogitatur, aliter cum id ipsum quod res est intelligitur. (i 103, 18f)	A thing is conceived in one way when it is the word describing it that is conceived, in another way when the thing itself is known.

The identification of the two possible *modi* of thinking (of the existence) of an object reminds us of a distinction which Anselm made and which we have already met. *Aliud est rem esse in intellectu, aliud intelligere rem esse* we heard in *Prosl.* 2[1] in the context of the introductory proof that there is at least an intramental existence of God.[2] We can think of an object by thinking of the word that describes it, that is by obeying the directions which our thinking receives from the sign language of this word and so considering what claims to be the thought of the object concerned. In that case we can and indeed we certainly will think of the object concerned as existing. We must first

[1] i 101, 9f.
[2] We must keep in mind here all that was said about the meaning of this statement and of its proof together with what was said in its defence against Gaunilo on pp. 108ff.

think of it as existing, even if we want to deny its existence, let
alone assert it. And precisely when it is the existence of God
that is in question, which is known to us by the *verbum praedicantium Christum*, the very first point will be to conceive the *vox
significans Deum*. There is no folly in that in itself. In *Prosl. 2*
Anselm constructed the first general form of his Proof on the
view that even the fool has to admit at least the intramental
existence of God and therefore to that extent cannot be a
fool: *quia hoc cum audit, intelligit; et quidquid intelligitur, in intellectu est*, just as an artist can and must see his work existing
in spirit before he has created it.[1] But of course this thinking
has as yet nothing to do with a real, objective, as distinct
from merely conceptual, existence or with knowledge of real
existence or therefore with Truth itself. For the truth of thinking or speaking stands or falls by the relations of its sign
language to what exists independently of its signs. Thinking of
the *vox significans rem* could only be true as an integrating
element in any thinking of the *res significata*.[2] The thinking of
the *vox significans rem* in itself, in abstraction from the thought of
something that really exists, or set over against it as something
different, would have to be described as false. Of course it
could still be an event possible and significant in itself. In that
case it would be false to call it 'wrong' in view of the meaning
or lack of meaning attaching to it because of the absence of
something that really exists.[3] The truth of a statement as such is

---

[1] I 101, 7ff and 14f.

[2] *Nihil est verum nisi participando veritatem; et ideo veri veritas in ipso vero est; res
vero enuntiata . . . causa veritatis eius (sc. enuntiationis) dicenda est* (De verit. 2: I 177,
16ff). Therefore it is not the *oratio* itself that is the *veritas*, but: *cum significat esse
quod est, tunc est in ea veritas et est vera*. In so far as such a *significatio recta est, non est
illi aliud veritas quam rectitudo* (ibid.: I 178, 6f, 16, 25). *Ad hoc namque nobis datum est
posse cogitare esse vel non esse aliquid, ut cogitemus esse quod est et non esse quod non est*
(ibid. *3:* I 180, 12ff).

[3] According to Anselm's doctrine of evil (*De casu diab. 19* [I 264] and *passim*;
De conc. virg. 4–5 [II 143–47]; *De concordia Qu. I 7* [II 257–60]) there is no evil *res*
or *actio* or *essentia* or *substantia*, but only an evil absence of *iustitia*, or *rectitudo*.
From this it follows for a doctrine of knowledge that any *significare esse quod non est*
is not outside of the truth of the natural powers (*cogitare posse*) and yet is false,
because the meaning of these powers is not satisfied thereby (*De verit. 2–3:* I
177–80).

linked with the fact that it has no permanence of its own. That means that as a statement it can be transitory and variable without its for that reason speaking any less truly.[1] Because this cannot be said of *cogitare vocem significantem* introduced in abstraction it is therefore false thinking; it is thus folly to think on this plane.

Illo itaque modo potest cogitari Deus non esse, isto vero minime. (I 103, 20)	In the first way, then, it is possible to think of God as not existing but impossible in the other.

The whole effort of *Prosl. 2-3* had been to prove conclusively that God cannot be conceived as not existing. The demonstration that this is impossible is Anselm's Proof of the Existence of God. The *insipiens* seems to confront him as living confutation of his proof: he can think of God as not existing.[2] Anselm does not deny this fact. Neither does he ascribe it to lack of intellectual capacity or to malevolent inconsistency on the part of the *insipiens*. But only to the simple fact that he is an *insipiens* and as such thinks on a level where one can only think falsely—though without violating the inner consistency of that level. When one thinks falsely, and from the foregoing that means directing one's thinking abstractly to the *vox significans rem* without knowing the *id ipsum quod res est*—as one must think as an *insipiens*—then it really is possible to do what according to the Proof of *Prosl. 2-3* is impossible. By the miracle of foolishness it is possible to think of God as not existing. But only by this miracle. Anselm had certainly not reckoned with this. His statement, and his proof of the statement, 'God cannot be

---

1 *Nulla igitur significatio est recta alia rectitudine quam illa, quae permanet pereunte significatione . . . Rectitudo, qua significatio recta dicitur, non habet esse aut aliquem motum per significationem quomodocumque ipsa moveatur significatio* (*De verit. 13:* I 198, 8f and 18ff). This definition results from the fact that in the last analysis God himself and only he is Truth, he who alone has permanence in himself: *Solius Dei est propriam habere voluntatem* (*Ep. de incarn. 10:* II 27, 11. Cf. *De casu diab. 4:* I 242, 5f). In the fundamental superiority of the *res* over against the *cogitatio*, or *significatio*, there is reflected God's superiority over all created reality.

2 It was not too paltry an objection for Gaunilo to raise it against Anselm: *Si non potest (sc. cogitari non ese): cur contra negantem aut dubitantem, quod sit aliqua talis natura, tota ista disputatio est assumpta?* (*Pro insip. 2:* I 126, 6f).

thought of as not existing' rests on the assumption of the *intelligere id ipsum quod res est*. His thinking is, as he admits, the thinking of *fides quaerens intellectum*. How could it think only the word 'God'? How could the word that is spoken to it about God be but an empty word? It starts out from the knowledge of God himself whose existence it wants to know. On this assumption God cannot possibly be thought of as not existing.

Nullus quippe intelligens id quod Deus est, potest cogitare quia Deus non est, licet haec verba dicat in corde, aut sine ulla aut cum aliqua extranea significatione. (1 103, 20–104, 2)	For no one who knows God himself can think, 'God does not exist'— even although he may say these words in his heart, whether without meaning or without relevance.

This is the presupposition of *fides quaerens intellectum* which cannot be abandoned even to please the *insipiens*, which, on the contrary rather, just because of the *insipiens*, has to be insisted upon to the end—if there is anything at all that can serve to make him cease from being a fool then it will be just this insistence—the presupposition on which the thought of God's non-existence is impossible: knowing God himself. That means: *intelligere id quod Deus est*. From the whole tenor of Anselm's thought and from what immediately follows it—*Deus enim est id quo maius cogitari non potest*—it cannot mean—'knowing God's Nature' so that God's existence would follow from what we know of his Nature.[1] It is certainly true that knowledge of

[1] According to the received Gerberon text our passage would run as follows: *nullus quippe intelligens id quod sunt ignis et aqua potest cogitare ignem esse aquam secundum rem; licet hoc possit secundum voces. Ita igitur nemo intelligens id quod Deus est, potest cogitare, quia Deus non est . . . (MPL* 158, 229). Thus: anyone who knows the Nature of fire and water, can so connect the corresponding terms that he brings about the meaningless thought 'water is fire'. But by that he does not think of anything real because it is contradictory to what we know of the nature of fire that it should be what we know as water. And so anyone who knows God's Nature can only conceive the terms and not the reality of God's non-existence, because non-existence is contrary to what we know is God's Nature. It cannot be put any better than Anselm has constantly tried to put it. But according to the textual studies of P. Daniels this whole picture of fire and water is an interpolation. W. von den Steinen who in the place already mentioned, p. 40, continually works with this picture, would certainly have held on to it. Anselm simply did not say what the old interpreter, and so many others after him, wanted to make him say. For him God and non-existence are of course so related, as fire and water are related, that it is impossible to predicate the one of the other. But the impossibility of God's non-existence is too unique a thing for it to be mentioned in the same breath as a

God's Nature, of his Omnipresence and Eternity, of his infinite Holiness and Mercy is also included in *intelligere id quod Deus est*. But the fact that it is this knowledge does not compel it to be knowledge of God's Existence too. Even if every conceivable physical and moral property were raised to the *n*th degree, that could quite well be nothing more than the sum total of the predicates of a purely conceptual being. The fact that *id quod Deus est* is synonomous with God himself makes this analogical, 'speculative' understanding of his reality into true knowledge of his Nature and that creates the fully efficacious, indeed over-efficacious substitute for the missing (and necessarily missing) experiential knowledge of him. This in turn compels knowledge of his Existence, the knowledge which is possible and becomes real so necessarily and so exclusively as against all other knowledge, including all denial and doubt, only in so far as it is knowledge of his Existence. God himself compels this knowledge. Whoever knows him himself cannot think, 'God does not exist'. No one has been able to do it who knew him. Wherever God has been known, he himself has excluded the very thought of this with mathematical precision, and wherever he is to be known, he will continue to exclude it. 'Exclude'—that means turn it into a thought that is impossible, null and void and finished. That we do from time to time actually think it, that from time to time with the fool we say in our heart 'there is no God'— as Anselm expressly takes into account—that is not excluded. At the very point where we are considering the compelling

comparison between fire and water. The impossibility of this latter comparison results from our knowledge of the nature of both. The impossibility of the non-existence of fire or of water would not result from that knowledge in itself. It results from it only in so far as our knowledge of the nature of both is experiential and is therefore knowledge that assumes their existence in fact. But it results only as an actual impossibility related to our experience. But on the one hand our knowledge of God's Nature is not that kind of experiential knowledge that actually presupposes God's Existence. And on the other hand, the impossibility of God's non-existence is not that kind of merely factual impossibility related to our experience. So it is possible—as this interpreter has done albeit in all sincerity and with great zeal— to consider oneself and conduct oneself as a pupil of Anselm and yet basically be a right good Gaunilo.

knowledge of God himself we have every reason to recall the solidarity, broken but not destroyed, that the man under this compulsion has with the *insipiens*. Perhaps, nay certainly, far more impassioned, far more complete and with far more doubt than is the case with the ordinary fool, will be the cry, 'there is no God', in the heart of him who knows God himself—we may think again here of Anselm's prayers which are not to be taken as mere rehetoric. But in the very act of thinking and uttering it, his denial will be cancelled and annulled. The words: 'God does not exist', will have no meaning in his mouth or in his heart or will have an alien meaning which has nothing at all to do with God himself whom he knows as existing, or with his knowledge of God or therefore with himself. He will not know what he is denying. He will be denying an idol. Or, he will be confessing his own abandonment of God, for it is just the man who knows God who will continually have reason to do this. But in no circumstances will he deny God himself. No more will he be able to form the thought, 'God (*id quod Deus est*, God himself) does not exist'. On no account—in so far as he knows God himself. Anselm developed his Proof on this level of *intelligere id quod Deus est*; it would have been senseless to have sought to develop it on any other level. Just for that reason the living embodiment in the *insipiens* of evidence to the contrary can make no material impression on him.

What the *insipiens* can prove is this and only this, that he does not know him whose Existence he denies. And it is not his denial, but his not knowing, that constitutes his folly.

Deus enim est id quo maius cogitari non potest. Quod qui bene intelligit, utique intelligit id ipsum sic esse, ut nec cogitatione queat non esse. Qui ergo intelligit sic esse Deum, nequit eum non esse cogitare. (I 104, 2ff)	For God is 'that beyond which nothing greater can be conceived'. Whoever truly knows that knows that it exists in such a way that even in thought it cannot but exist. And so whoever knows that this is the manner of God's existence cannot conceive him as not existing.

What does it mean to know—to know and recognize—God

himself? Anselm goes back to his *argumentum*. God is he who, revealing himself as Creator, is called *quo maius cogitari nequit* and therefore who immediately confronts us with his Name as the one who forbids us to conceive a greater than him. To know that properly is to know *id quod Deus est*, God himself. In this his Name as Lord he himself is and is known, known in such a way that the denial of his Existence becomes impossible and thereby the proof of his Existence is made valid. Therefore *bene intelligere* is not to be immediately equated *a priori* with *intelligere id ipsum quod res est*. But in the sense of our passage *bene intelligere* is the fulfilment, the development, the manner of this real knowledge, which by its relation to the object establishes itself as true. It consists concretely in the fact that the embargo contained in the Name of God is heard, recognized and obeyed and that therefore in his thinking man allows God to be God. In his very thoughts, precisely in the limitation of his freedom of thought. All piety and morality are nothing worth, have nothing to do with God and can even be atheistic or may become atheistic again unless they are directed towards establishing an absolute limitation on this, the most inward and most intimate area of freedom. *Bene intelligere* means: to know once and for all, as a real ox knows its master or a true ass its master's stall. *Bene intelligere* means: finally to realize that it is not possible to think beyond God, not possible to think as a spectator of oneself or of God, that all thinking about God has to begin with thinking to God. That is what the fool and also his advocate Gaunilo have not yet realized. Those who have realized it, by so doing, stand under the compulsion of knowledge of God's Existence. And immediately and primarily of that existence of God which belongs only to him amongst all that exists, his *sic esse*, the existence which cannot be annulled even in mere thought. Once more and with no ambiguity Anselm makes clear that the narrowed-down Proof of *Prosl. 3*, the proof of this *sic esse*, the proof that it is impossible for God to be conceived as not existing, is what he understands by knowledge and proof of God's Existence. With the *bene intelligere* of the divine Name a 'God' who as God can be conceived as not existing is cast out and room made for the God of faith, of revelation and of the Church who so exists that he makes even the thought of his non-existence impossible. To know God himself, as the fool does not know him, means therefore to stand under the compulsion of this his Existence. Therefore those who know God himself, the *intelligens id quod Deus est*, cannot conceive of God as not existing.

Gratias tibi, bone Domine, gratias tibi, quia quod prius credidi te donante, iam sic intelligo te illuminante, ut si te esse nolim credere, non possim non intelligere. (I 104, 5ff)	I thank thee, good Lord, I thank thee, that what I at first believed because of thy gift, I now know because of thine illumining in such a way that even if I did not want to believe thine Existence, yet I could not but know it.

The Proof as Anselm wanted to conduct it and had to conduct it is finished. He himself reminds us again of what he understands by proof. Not a science that can be unravelled by the Church's faith and that establishes the Church's faith in a source outside of itself. It is a question of theology. It is a question of the proof of faith by faith which was already established in itself without proof. And both—faith that is proved and faith that proves—Anselm expressly understands not as presuppositions that can be achieved by man but as presuppositions that have been achieved by God, the former as divine *donare* and the latter as divine *illuminare*. He 'assumed'[1] neither the Church's *Credo* nor his own *credere*, but he prayed and the Church's *Credo* and his own *credere* were assumed. God gave himself to him to know and he was able to know God. On this foundation, comparable to no philosophical presupposition and inconceivable for all systematic theology, he has come to know and has proved the Existence of God. For that reason his last word must be gratitude. Not satisfaction over a work that he has completed and that resounds to his

[1] Cf. p. 153, n. 1.

own praise as its master, but gratitude for a work that has been done and of which he is in no sense the master.

God gave himself as the object of his knowledge and God illumined him that he might know him as object. Apart from this event there is no proof of the existence, that is of the reality of God. But in the power of this event there is a proof which is worthy of gratitude. It is truth that has spoken and not man in search of faith. Man might not want faith. Man might remain always a fool. As we heard, it is of grace if he does not. But even if he did, *si te esse nolim credere*, truth has spoken—in a way that cannot be ignored, refuted or forgotten and in such a way that man is forbidden and to that extent is unable not to recognize it. Just because it is the science of faith about faith, theology possesses light but it is not the light of the theologian's faith.

That Anselm's Proof of the Existence of God has repeatedly been called the 'Ontological' Proof of God, that commentators have refused to see that it is in a different book altogether from the well-known teaching of Descartes[1] and Leibniz,[2] that anyone could seriously think that it is even remotely affected by what Kant put forward against these doctrines[3]—all that is so much nonsense on which no more words ought to be wasted.

[1] *Discours de la méthode* IV; *Médit.* III and V.   [2] *Monadologie* 45.
[3] *Kritik der reinen Vernunft* 2nd ed., pp. 625f.

INDEX

The figures in italics refer to footnotes